Praise

How to Act Like a Christian

A book on acting like a Christian ought to be wise, clear, and hands-on helpful. This one is! I liked it so much, I will give copies to my adult children.

—*Dr. Jerry Sheveland, President, Baptist General Conference*

That road from believer to fully devoted follower of Jesus Christ is carrying more traffic than ever before in American history. What are the questions and concerns those pilgrims bring to church? This book articulates the concerns and also includes tested and relevant responses.

—*Lyle E. Schaller, Parish Consultant*

Leith's book provides a practical, step-by-step anatomy lesson for understanding and learning the basics of daily Christian life. What makes this book invaluable is its well-targeted, proactive guidance on tricky subjects for Christians like making decisions, dealing with criticism, and living through loss and illness. Well done!

—*Sue Nilson Kibbey, Executive Pastor, Ginghamsburg Church*

"I was in the midst of making a very important and life changing career decision when I encountered the *How To Act Like a Christian* series. Specifically, the chapter that addressed "Making Important Decisions" gave me an insightful framework to help me make what has proven to be a wonderful decision directed by God."

—*Jill Fox, Wooddale Church*

"I became a Christian near the beginning of the *How to Act like a Christian* series. Several of the topics ignited weekly conversations with my friends and family that guided me through important life issues. Specifically (and poignantly) my fiancé and I learned about making godly choices in our finances and setting important sexual boundaries prior to our upcoming wedding."

—*Jeff Smith, Wooddale Church*

HOW TO ACT LIKE A CHRISTIAN

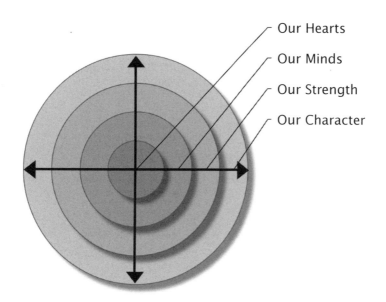

Our Hearts

Our Minds

Our Strength

Our Character

HOW TO ACT LIKE A CHRISTIAN

Leith Anderson

Abingdon Press
Nashville

HOW TO ACT LIKE A CHRISTIAN

Copyright © 2006 Leith Anderson

All rights reserved.

This book is printed on recycled, acid-free paper.

Library of Congress Cataloging-in-Publication Data

Anderson, Leith, 1944-
   How to act like a Christian / Leith Anderson.
      p. cm.
   Includes bibliographical references.
   ISBN 0-687-33555-8 (alk. paper)
   1. Christian life. I. Title.

   BV4501.3.A535 2006
   248.4--dc22

                                                    2006013754

06 07 08 09 10 11 12 13 14 15—10 09 08 07 06 05 04 03 02 01

MANUFACTURED IN THE UNITED STATES OF AMERICA

Contents

Part One:
The Christian Heart...Putting Love into Action 9

Chapter One: Loving Like a Saint 11

Chapter Two: Forgiving Those who Sin Against Us 19

Chapter Three: Caring Enough to Share the Very Best 29

Part Two:
The Christian Mind...Imitating the Mind of Christ 39

Chapter Four: Managing Money Like God is Going to Ask 41

Chapter Five: Setting Sexual Boundaries 51

Chapter Six: Making Important Decisions 61

Part Three:
Christian Strength...Persevering through Difficulty . 69

Chapter Seven: Coping with Criticism 71

Chapter Eight: Facing Serious Illness 81

Chapter Nine: Grieving Great Losses 91

Part Four:
Christian Character...
Growing in the Hallmarks of Faith 101

Chapter Ten: Living with a Purpose in Life 103

Chapter Eleven: Praying that Makes a Difference 113

Chapter Twelve: Holding on to Hope 125

Chapter Thirteen: Walking by Faith 135

Appendix: Index of Hope 145
Notes 151

Part One:
The Christian Heart...
Putting Love into
Action

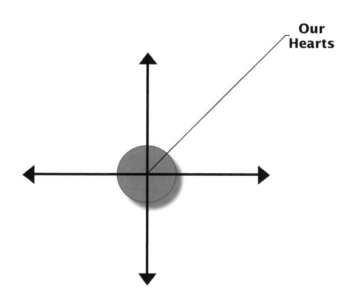

Our
Hearts

Chapter One

Loving Like a Saint

Under General George Washington, the patriots were an inadequate military force against the greatest army in the world—the army of Great Britain, famous for their red coats.

The American patriots couldn't even afford uniforms, let alone adequate provisions and firearms. Sometimes they went into battle without even shoes. The troops needed something that would identify them, so Washington's army would wear something different into every battle. Sometimes it was a ribbon, sometimes it was a twig that was stuck into their clothing, but there was always a marker so they would know who belonged to the American forces.[1]

Jesus Christ did something similar for all of those who became his followers. He didn't order a red coat or a yellow ribbon, but he did give an instruction on how Christians could be easily identified. Jesus said, *"A new command I give you: Love one another. As I have loved you, so you must love one another. By this everyone will know that you are my disciples, if you love one another"* (John 13:34-35).

So love is the distinguishing characteristic of Christians. You can always identify followers of Jesus by the love that they show. If this is the sign by which people know us, then we need to learn how to be good at loving like saints.

Is it as easy as just *deciding* to love others? How does this actually work?

Former President Jimmy Carter tells the story of a Cuban immigrant pastor named Eloy Cruz, a man who focused his life and ministry on Puerto Rican immigrants to the United States, people who were among the poorest of the poor. President Carter asked this pastor about the secret of his success. Cruz responded in humility and with a certain measure of embarrassment. "Señor Jimmy, we only need to have two loves in life—for God and for the person who happens to be standing in front of us at any time."[2]

These "two loves" are well summarized in 1 John 4:7-21:

Dear friends, let us love one another, for love comes from God. Everyone who loves has been born of God and knows God. Whoever does not love does not know God, because God is love. This is how God showed his love among us. He sent his one and only Son into the world that we might live through him. This is love: not that we loved God, but that he loved us and sent his Son as an atoning sacrifice for our sins. Dear friends, since God so loved us, we also ought to love one another. No one has ever seen God; but if we love one another, God lives in us and his love is made complete in us. This is how we know that we live in him and he in us: He has given us of his Spirit. And we have seen and testify that the Father has sent his Son to be the Savior of the world. If anyone acknowledges that Jesus is the Son of God, God lives in them and they in God. And so we know and rely on the love God has for us. God is love. Whoever lives in love lives in God, and God in them. This is how love is made complete among us so that we will have confidence on the day of judgment: In this world we are like Jesus. There is no fear in love. But perfect love drives out fear, because fear has to do with punishment. The one who fears is not made perfect in love. We love because he first loved us. If we say we love God yet hate a brother or sister, we are liars. For if we do not love a fellow believer, whom we have seen, we cannot love God whom we have not seen. And he has given us this command: Those who love God must also love one another.

Here we have the mother lode of biblical teaching about loving others, and it really can be summed up very simply. God loves us; we love God and others.

That's easy to say—and as anyone who has tried to do this unconditionally knows—hard to do. Perhaps we need some guidelines.

Principle #1: Just do it

To be a Christian is to be a lover. There's been much misunderstanding about this, because often we think of love primarily as an emotion—something we have to *feel* toward someone else. Of course there is a dimension of love that *is* emotional. However, the biblical definition of love is *action that is in the best interest of another person*. Love is bent toward action.

I would never say, "Go ahead and hate everybody; just make sure you *act* like you love them." That's not what the Bible tells us to do. But if it comes down to a stand off between how you feel and what you do, biblical love is more about action than feelings. It would be ideal to combine them both in all of their fullness so that you felt an emotional love toward somebody while demonstrating love through action. But those things don't always come to us as a set. Christians love others whether they feel like it or not. Love is action—*doing.*

So do something! Show your Christian love. When somebody is standing in front of you, whoever that person is, react with the loving action that comes to mind. Just do it. The goal is to get into the habit. When you start a healthy, new life change—exercising, eating better, reading your Bible daily—it's difficult at first. You do it once and it's just plain hard. You do it twice and it's still difficult. You do it ten times and you start planting the seeds of a habit. At a hundred times, the habit will be established. Just start doing it.

"Okay," you say, "but what if I don't *feel* like it? What if I mess up? Here's a person whom I don't even like, and I'm supposed to act as if I love them? What's that going to do? I'm going to come across as a complete hypocrite."

Does it help to know that you are not the only person to face the embarrassment of difficult love? David Yonggi Cho is a pastor and the founder of a church in Seoul, Korea that is said to be the largest church in the world with 750,000 members. He is a marvelous communicator and in great demand around the world as a speaker. Pastor Yonggi Cho actually told God he would be willing to go anywhere in the world as a representative of Jesus Christ—except Japan. He had a good reason for this: the deep animosity that he and other Koreans felt toward the Japanese people because of atrocities committed during World War II. In Pastor Yonggi Cho's case there was family experience with these atrocities.

So, of course, he was invited to speak to 1,000 Christian pastors in the country of Japan. He accepted the invitation because he knew that it was the right thing to do, but he didn't want to go. Pastor Yonggi Cho prepared what he was going to say, stood up, looked at this audience of a thousand, and what came out of his mouth was absolutely not what he had prepared. He said, "I hate you. I hate you. I hate you." Good start for Christian love!? When he realized what he had said, he broke down and cried in front of all those people. Watching him weep, one person stood and then another and then another. One by one, a thousand people came to the front of the auditorium and asked him for forgiveness. It was such a stirring experience that at the end of it, he looked at them and said, "I love you. I love you. I love you." His attempt to express Christian love in a difficult circumstance was a bit shaky, but he got started.[3]

Take heart. In this challenge of Christian love, we are not alone. There are thousands, perhaps millions, of fellow Christians who are also taking steps to get better at expressing the love of Jesus. The Spirit of God is engaged with us. God is in us. We merely need to get started and do it. We'll be amazed at what God will add in value to our efforts.

Principle #2: Start small

When it comes to loving as a Christian, teachers may encourage us to start really big. The challenge sounds something like this (I've probably said this myself!): "Think of the person whom you most hate in the whole world. Yes, think of that person who did you in, wounded you deeply, and betrayed your trust. There isn't another person you resent as much as this one individual. All right, this week go out and love them."

I don't know what that does for you, but it makes me feel guilty and rotten. I'm quite sure that most of us, if forced into this situation, would fail the test.

When we hear the story of an enormous, overwhelming act of love it only makes us feel even more inadequate. For example, I read a story of amazing heroism and love that occurred during the Battle for Fallujah. It was November 15, 2004, and a United States Marine was in an enclosed area when a fragmentation grenade was thrown in. He grabbed the grenade and cradled it to himself. When the grenade exploded, the marine lost his life, but he saved the lives of his comrades. [4] When confronted with stories like that, I fear that if I were in those circumstances, I would behave very differently. I fear I would not measure up to the standard of Sergeant Raphael Peralto.

So take off the table this business of first trying to love the most difficult person in our lives. Let's remove from our list any extreme acts of heroism. Instead of starting with the hardest people, let's start loving the easiest people. Who's the easiest person you can think of to love? And what is the smallest thing that can be done as an expression of Christian love? Start there.

Principle #3: Start with Christians

When you're just starting out with this behavior, you might find it easier to love fellow Christians. You may immediately think of a few exceptions to this notion, but, overall, it will probably be easier to begin expressing your love to those who are followers of Christ. Jesus said that's the way it's supposed to be. *"Dear friends, let us love one another...*" (1 John 4:7). Love is the mark we wear each day, just as the American soldiers in 1776 wore a mark when they went into battle. Practice. Practice on Christians. View another Christian as a target for your Christian love, and follow through. Pick any believer you want and target them with shots of love.

Get out there and do it!

You may have all kinds of great ideas. Good for you. That's wonderful. But others of us really wish that we had ideas to implement right away without thinking too much. Here are a few concrete exercises.

Smile. That's fairly simple and a quick place to begin. We can wonderfully bless other people with a smile.

Some people are natural smilers. I am married to one. My wife Charleen's face at rest is friendly. But I'm not a natural smiler. My face at rest is neutral (at best) and sometimes grouchy. I can be absolutely happy and content, and yet those feelings don't show on my face. I have to work at smiling. Sometimes I have to think things through and make myself do it. It doesn't seem as natural and as good as some people who are natural smilers, but it gets easier.

Give it a try. Right now. Practice smiling.

How did that feel? Strange? Unnatural? Keep practicing. Smile into the mirror. If you really want to ease into this, do it on the phone.

When you've mastered that, go out into public. Look someone in the eye and smile. If you don't have the courage to do that at first, smile at someone who you know will smile back—an acquaintance or a friend. Now branch out. Try strangers. Find someone who is not smiling and target him. See if by smiling you can actually get him to crack a smile, too. Don't get carried away, but make it part of every day. If it still doesn't feel natural, go back to practicing. Try it ten times. Branch out. Try smiling at work. Show Christian love with an intentional smile.

Practice giving. It's another way to show Christian love. I was in a downtown McDonald's, in the line near the cash register. Ahead of me was a mom with her little child. I could sense that she was ordering very carefully to make sure that she got the most for her money. She opened her wallet, and I snooped. I looked over her shoulder to see how much was there. She had a few dollar bills and coins. She counted out the coins to pay for the food. At the next register was another woman, who I could best describe as a bag lady. Her clothes were dirty, her hair was disheveled, and she was being even more careful with her purchase. She made an order, but as she counted the coins onto the counter, she didn't have enough. I watched as this single mom reached into her wallet, took out her singles, and passed them, low down under the counter, into the hand of the woman next to her so no one else would see. Nothing was said, but I caught the glance and saw what was in that woman's eyes as she looked up at the mom who had given her the gift. That's giving. It's a simple, profound, and spontaneous act of Christian love.

Giving can be habit-forming. Jesus said that giving is more blessed than receiving. It's the better end of the deal. Christians who start giving get hooked on it. Give, and you receive the blessing. You want to do it more and more until it becomes an addiction.

Encourage. Encouragement is one of the very best expressions of Christian love, and it is something that everyone needs. How important is it?

Dan Baber posted encouragement for sale on eBay. He promised that the person with the highest bid would receive an e-mail from his mother, Sue Hamilton, which would make the recipient feel like the most special person in the world. The starting minimum bid: one dollar. You are probably thinking what I thought: "Who would pay to receive an encouraging e-mail?" It turns out that there were 42,711 hits and 92 cash bids. The winning bid was $610. If you are now thinking of posting encouraging notes for sale on eBay, may God forgive you, because that is not the point! The anecdote demonstrates how much we want and need encouragement. Some people are willing to pay over $600 to be encouraged.[5]

So here's your challenge: Send an e-mail to somebody this week—an e-mail that she won't delete because the thoughts you express are exactly what she needed to hear. Send a letter on stationery that will be read again and again. Leave a voice mail message of encouragement for somebody that will be saved because the recipient is touched by your thoughtfulness and kindness. Or just walk up to somebody face-to-face and build him up. Encouragement is love in action, an expression of Christian love.

Count the opportunities

What do you think about before you go to sleep at night? Some people fall asleep in three minutes or less. I'm one of them. Other people have to work at getting sleepy for two or three hours before actually falling asleep. Yet in those moments or hours, we all think. In bed tonight, don't count sheep. Think about ways that you expressed Christian love today and count them. Think about ways that you can express Christian love tomorrow. Put yourself to sleep thinking about what is possible if your loving action gets into full swing.

Find a symbol to remind yourself to deliberately love others. Perhaps you'll come across a small, heart-shaped rock to put on your desk at work. Cut out a paper heart and tape it in the window. Hang a heart painting in your home. Wear a heart necklace. Every time you see the heart symbol, remind yourself to love like a Christian. Find a way to remember daily that love identifies you as a follower of Jesus Christ.

Next time you're listening to a song about love, let it motivate you to go out and express Christian love to whomever crosses your path. Put into regular practice Jesus' words: "*By this everyone will know that you are my disciples if you love one another*" (John 13:35).

Chapter Two

Forgiving Those who Sin Against Us

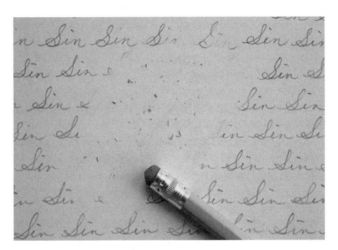

Some people don't like to forgive.

That's the way it was with a man named Harry. His wife, Wilma, offended him one day, so he stopped talking to her as punishment. The silent treatment lasted for a week until one Sunday when Harry needed Wilma's help. He was scheduled for an early Monday flight to go on a business trip. The clock radio was on his wife's side of the bed so he wrote her a note that read, "Wake me up at 4:15 AM."

Shortly after 8 AM on Monday Harry awakened by himself. There was a note waiting for him on Wilma's pillow that said, "It's 4:15 AM. Wake up!"

Harry should have found a better way.

Joseph, whose story is found in the book of Genesis, took a very different approach. His family problem was much more than a minor marital spat. His older brothers hated him so much that they conspired to murder him. In a last minute compromise, one of his brothers suggested that they sell him instead. He was carried off to a foreign country as a slave, a common practice in those days. They intended this to be a living death for their younger brother. Whether or not you're familiar with the story from the last chapters of Genesis or the Broadway play, *Joseph and the Amazing Technicolor Dreamcoat,* you know that life was hard for this young, Jewish man who was enslaved in Egypt. Imagine his loneliness, sense of betrayal, and shock. He had gone from being the pampered son of a large family to an overworked slave in a foreign land, due to the deliberate actions of his own brothers.

Things couldn't get worse for this young man, right? Wrong. Despite a stellar record of service to his new owner, he was falsely accused of sexual assault and imprisoned. While locked away and suffering extreme deprivation, what went through his mind? Did he wonder, "Why me?" Did he think bitterly about his brothers and the misery they had caused him?

The Bible doesn't record his state of mind. All we know is that God rewarded Joseph's continued faithfulness, despite his circumstances. Eventually he was pardoned and rose in influence to become prime minister of Egypt. He became one of the most successful and powerful leaders of his generation. He was human, though, so we can assume that even as a busy, well-respected politician with power and new affluence, he still carried those memories with him. Perhaps, to cope, he buried them deep in the back of his mind. But the nightmarish images of his brothers' treachery must have come back vividly when—in the midst of a terrible famine—his family migrated to Egypt seeking food. Joseph was about to be confronted with his past and challenged to respond with either hatred or forgiveness. The story climaxes in Genesis 50 when the brothers feared Joseph's likely and well-deserved revenge.

> *When Joseph's brothers saw that their father was dead, they said, "What if Joseph holds a grudge against us and pays us back for all the wrongs we did to him?" So they sent word to Joseph, saying, "Your father left these instructions before he died: 'This is what you are to say to Joseph: I ask you to forgive your brothers the sins and the wrongs they committed in treating you so badly.' Now please forgive*

*the sins of the servants of the God of your father." When
their message came to him, Joseph wept. His brothers then
came and threw themselves down before him. "We are your
slaves," they said.* (Genesis 50:15-18)

What a bunch of unrepentant, lying hypocrites! These brothers
never admitted doing anything wrong. They didn't apologize.
They made up a message from their dead father telling Joseph
to forgive them. Years had passed, and they were still behaving
badly—and Joseph knew it.

So, what was Joseph's response? Put yourself in his spot and
imagine *your* response. Now read his words.

*Joseph said to them, "Don't be afraid. Am I in the place
of God? You intended to harm me, but God intended it for
good to accomplish what is now being done, the saving
of many lives. So then, don't be afraid. I will provide for
you and your children." And he reassured them and spoke
kindly to them.* (Genesis 50:19-21)

Joseph lived more than a thousand years before Jesus and
before anyone would be called a Christian, but when it came to
forgiving those who sinned against him, he acted like one.

We can identify with Joseph

None of us is likely to be sold into Egyptian slavery by our
siblings, but we can identify with the disappointment and hurt
that Joseph experienced because of the actions of others. Every
day we suffer scores of small offenses while driving around
town, attending school, and living at home. Sure, these events
are little things; even so, they may be painful wrongs that we
must work to overcome and forget.

Then there are the big issues. Many of us have been deeply
hurt by the significant and devastating sins of others. Some
have had our lives and hearts scarred by sexual assault, domes-
tic abuse, business deceit, racial discrimination, lying, theft,
and even the murder of family members or friends. The list of

terrible possibilities and realities is long. When we suffer a serious wrong, the trauma is a vivid, raw, and very real part of our lives. What can a Christian do? What is a realistic and healing response?

Opening the door: thinking about forgiving

Jesus taught his followers—his disciples and us—to pray for forgiveness of our sins just as we forgive those who sin against us (the Lord's Prayer, Matthew 6:9-13), but when we are thinking about the major transgressions of others, that simple task can seem huge, baffling, and even impossible. How do we begin to accomplish such an enormous task? Jesus said that Christians must forgive, so perhaps we need to start the process by thinking about what forgiving is and isn't.

Forgiving is a choice. When someone hurts us, we get to decide whether to hold a grudge and seek revenge or to forgive. Involved in that choice is a mixture of emotions. Initially we *feel* this choice more than we can dispassionately think about it; but, sooner or later, forgiving always comes down to what we *choose* to do.

Forgiving is seldom easy. It may be relatively simple for you to forgive the thousands of tiny irritations that are part of your daily life, but it is almost never easy to forgive people who have hurt our feelings, treated us with disrespect, or caused us injury. Forgiving is often very hard work.

Forgiving is letting go. The basic meaning of the word *forgive* is to "give up." To forgive is to quit, surrender, and let go of hurt, anger, and the desire to keep score or get even. To forgive is to move on and leave what happened behind. That means no more obsessing, mulling over, or focusing energy on what happened and who did it.

Think of your life as a large warehouse where you have all kinds of activities occurring at once. The trouble is that you've given 50 percent of your floor space to what happened when you were growing up or in an abusive relationship. The memories, anger, and bitterness have taken over your life and your thinking. Potential good is being crowded out. To forgive is to stop renting space to the bad thing that happened and the person responsible.

Forgiving is about the future not just the past. When we consider forgiving, we usually think about what happened yesterday, but forgiveness is very much about tomorrow. The pain, anger, and distress we are currently experiencing is hurting us *right now*. No matter what happened in the past, there is nothing we can do to change history. Forgiving is about the future and how we are going to live it.

Forgiving is good for us. Researchers are discovering that forgiving lowers blood pressure, heart rate, muscle tension, and sweat gland activity. Lack of forgiving may compromise the immune system.[6] Forgiving is good for our bodies, relationships, families, churches, and communities. Forgiving is good for us all.

Forgiving is freeing. Carrying around grudges, resentment, hurt, and anger can be a huge burden. Think of everyone and everything you haven't forgiven. Picture each incident or person as a rock. Little ones are pebbles, and big ones are boulders. Take an imaginary marker and write a name, event, and date on each rock. Imagine carrying these rocks on your back all day and sleeping with them at night. Unforgiven offenses can be a terrible burden. When we forgive, there is enormous new freedom.

Forgiving is like God. God is the great forgiver. Although God has suffered great wrongs, more than we can fathom, we read repeatedly in the Bible that God loves us regardless of our offenses. God is willing to forgive—in a heartbeat, at a moment's notice, wholeheartedly, and without reservation. God's absolute willingness to forgive is embodied and personified in Jesus, God's son, whom he sent to earth to die as a substitute for us, the ones who sinned. While suffering terrible pain on the cross, Jesus even prayed that God would forgive his executioners! He said, "Father, forgive them, for they do not know what they are doing" (Luke 23:34). If Jesus was able to do that, it is no surprise that we, his followers, are to: *"Bear with each other and*

23

forgive one another if any of you has a grievance against some-one. Forgive as the Lord forgave you" (Colossians 3:13).

Forgiving is not forgetting or condoning. To forgive is not to endorse, condone, or approve what an offender has done. For-giveness is about you and your obedience to God.

Forgiving is not reconciliation. Being willing to forgive does not mean that everything will return to the way it was before the offense. It does not mean that a victim of abuse must welcome the abuser back home. It does not mean that criminals should be set free. The consequences of an offense don't disappear when one is forgiven.

Forgiving is not always quick. We can't always expect instant forgiveness from people who have endured life-altering hurts. Rape, incest, robbery, arson, and murder cannot be placed in the same category with the lesser offenses that are part of everyone's life. Christians have forgiven horrific sins, and sometimes they have done so quickly. God gives us the ability to forgive any crime against us, but he doesn't say that forgive-ness is guaranteed to be instantaneous when we have been deeply injured. In some cases, it will take special effort and the help of the Holy Spirit to extend forgiveness an inch at a time. There can be setbacks—ten steps forward followed by a few steps back. It is a process.

Starting the process: forgiving sins against us

The Bible makes it clear that Christians are called to forgive. How do we begin what can seem like a Herculean task?

Start with prayer. Even before deciding or trying to forgive, pray and talk to God. Pray the Lord's Prayer, thinking particu-larly about the line that reminds us how we should forgive so God will forgive us. Boldly ask God for wisdom, strength, and help. Starting with God is what Christians do. Otherwise, we are merely going through a psychological exercise. To make forgiv-ing a supernatural experience, commit the process to God and ask God to help you act like a Christian as you deal with your hurt and anger. If you're having trouble finding the words, try this sample prayer: "God, you know what happened. You know how you want me to handle this. I need your help. I don't know if I can forgive, but I am starting the process by committing this to you. Help me in Jesus' name. Amen."

Name that sin. Don't skip this step! Name the sin that stands between you and forgiveness. Be absolutely specific. Who did what when? What was sinful about what happened? Why were you and are you offended? This is important because many of us carry vague memories of past offenses along with general ill will toward people who have hurt us. Unless we force ourselves to articulate the offense, we are unable to forgive the offense. Sometimes we discover that there is no actual offense to forgive. So, say what is bothering you; state what was done wrong; specifically name that sin!

Tell someone. It may be helpful to select one or two trustworthy Christian friends (who can absolutely keep a confidence) and tell them who has offended you and how. Do this carefully. Don't let it be a gripe session or gossip attack. Telling a wise friend can give you another perspective, verify the reality of the offense, and help you practice getting it out in the open. Ask this godly person to pray for you and the person or people involved.

Choose to forgive. The act of forgiving finally comes down to an act of the will. We must decide if we are willing to forgive or not. We must choose. Bear in mind that choosing to forgive is not the same as forgiving, but it is an important step. Making up our minds frees us to take the next step of finding a way, with God's help, to actually forgive and let go.

Be practical

Every situation is different. Think and pray about the best way for you to grant Christian forgiveness. Sometimes the process requires a face-to-face conversation with the offender. Sometimes it is better to forgive without confronting. Sometimes the forgiveness must be granted to a person who has disappeared or died. The apostle Paul gives us some guidelines that can be summarized like this: do the very best you can to do what is right and make peace. You can then leave the final outcome in the hands of God.

Beware of projecting your expectations on others. One of the reasons many of us are offended and struggle to forgive is that we create expectations for others that we cannot enforce. We expect the boss to give a raise, the in-laws to change their traditions, the church to solve our problems, the criminal to make restitution, or the neighbor to be friendly. Then we are disappointed and offended because others don't meet our expectations and frustrated because we can't get them to do so. Be reasonable and understanding. We cannot enforce our standards on the behavior of others. We cannot control their actions. We only need to be responsible for ourselves.

Do good. A powerful tool in the Christian toolbox of forgiving is to do good to those who have sinned against us. Impossible? That's what Joseph did. His brothers hated him, treated him cruelly, tried to kill him, and sold him into slavery. Rather than retaliate, Joseph empathized and gave them food, land, and protection when they were in desperate need. He forgave *and* did good. This is a solid biblical principle.

> *Do not repay anyone evil for evil. Be careful to do what is right in the eyes of everyone. If it is possible, as far as it depends on you, live at peace with everyone. Do not take revenge, my dear friends, but leave room for God's wrath, for it is written: "It is mine to avenge; I will repay," says the Lord.* (Romans 12:17-19)

Don't get even with animosity and hatred. Repay evil with generosity and love. Make forgiving an action rather than merely a mental decision.

Reinterpret yesterday. You can take one more practical action toward forgiveness by reinterpreting the past. This is both biblically based and psychologically healthy.

When we are offended, we often feel like victims who have lost control. There is a sense that neither God is nor we are in charge of our lives but that we have been overpowered by the behavior and words of those who have hurt us. We are overwhelmed. The lingering feelings can last years after the offense.

When we forgive, we find that God has empowered us and we have taken back the control. We have made a choice that the offender cannot control. Now we can see yesterday differently. We have changed from victims to heroes. We have done what is right even when someone else has done wrong. We have acted with God even if the perpetrator has acted against God. Through forgiveness, we can replace sadness with happiness.[7]

Remember Joseph. He *"reassured...and spoke kindly"* to the brothers who, by every human standard, deserved his retribution. But Joseph refused to become a victim of that kind of bitterness. He listened to God. He replaced his own sadness with the joy of serving his Lord.

Forgiven, now forgiving

As Christians, asked to forgive the unforgivable, we don't go alone or first. We follow God, the one who first forgave us. Following God's example, we forgive others. It's all part of God's plan, and it's one more way we can grow. It's one more way we can truly act like a Christian.

> *Therefore, as God's chosen people, holy and dearly loved, clothe yourselves with compassion, kindness, humility, gentleness and patience. Bear with each other and forgive one another if any of you has a grievance against someone. Forgive as the Lord forgave you (Colossians 3:12-13).*

Chapter Three

Caring Enough to Share the Very Best

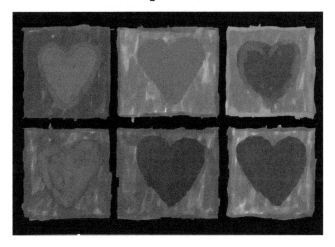

Imagine having the cure to cancer in your grasp, or a way to solve the problem of world hunger forever. Picture a public policy or campaign that would reduce child abuse by staggering numbers. Envision redesigning and retraining society so that racial discrimination in this country would be wiped out forever. Imagine having that kind of power for good. Would you keep your plans to yourself? Impossible! You'd want to share your plan, get it implemented, and see all of the positive objectives that could be accomplished in your lifetime. You'd be eager to let people know because some things are too important to keep quiet. That's exactly how it is to be in possession of the news about Jesus Christ. When you have that kind of message, you know it's too important not to share.

Well, somebody must be talking. Jesus started out with just a handful of followers, and today there are approximately two billion people around the world who call themselves Christians.[8] Those early believers shared their stories and their faith with others who then chose to follow Jesus, too.

Evangelism—telling others about the faith that has changed our lives—is characteristic of Christians. We take the time (and sometimes the courage) to explain the gospel of Jesus Christ, sharing what it means and what it can do for others. Some of us cling to an old image that evangelism is something that missionaries do, not us. The truth is that everyone who calls himself or herself a Christian is a missionary, an emissary with a message. To be a Christian is to act in ways that make others want to be Christians. (It's not just about what we say!) Christians evangelize.

Yet, some of us are embarrassed and reluctant. We don't share the message contained in the gospel accounts of Jesus' life for a variety of reasons: we aren't convinced that we have the gift, we don't know how; we don't want to offend anyone, or we're simply afraid to try. But no matter how we look at this issue, we keep coming back to the core truth: some things are too important *not* to share.

Why share your faith?

Let's keep our starter list of reasons for Christians to share our faith short and simple (although we could surely add dozens more):

Reason #1: Jesus says so. When we become Christians, we give our allegiance to Jesus. He becomes the Lord of our lives, which means that he becomes the boss. We state our belief that he is God's Son, we agree that through him lies the possibility of a relationship with our creator, and we promise to follow his teachings. Even if there were no other reason to speak to others about our faith in Jesus, Christians who are committed to him would not be able to keep this news quiet.

Here are Jesus' words: *"Go and make disciples of all nations, baptizing them in the name of the Father and of the Son and of the Holy Spirit, and teaching them to obey everything I have commanded you"* (Matthew 28:19-20). His command compels us. His example inspires us. This is Jesus himself giving us instructions. Jesus expected every Christian to join in reaching new believers who would be authentic disciples—people who are Christian in more than name only, who live out the faith, and who learn and obey what Jesus commanded while he was on earth.

Reason #2: People are lost. This is not a popular notion in a culture that says that people are generally good, everyone is headed to heaven, and every religion is a way to get there. The New Testament, however, is clear that Jesus is the only way to salvation. Without his supernatural help, people are lost from God.

Jesus said, *"I am the way and the truth and the life. No one comes to the Father except through me"* (John 14:6). So there it is in a nutshell, a hard-to-face reality but one that is central to the Christian faith.

This pointed message, however, has a happy ending. Look at the good news that comes in John 3:16: *"God so loved the world that he gave his one and only Son, that whoever believes in him shall not perish but have eternal life."* Don't stop reading there. Keep going to see the rest of what Jesus taught about those who don't believe.

> *For God did not send his Son into the world to condemn the world, but to save the world through him. Whoever believes in him is not condemned, but whoever does not believe stands condemned already because they have not believed in the name of God's one and only Son. (John 3:17-18)*

Jesus is the way. It's that simple. He leaves no room for us to misunderstand him. You'll find reminders throughout the New Testament. Read Acts 4:12: *"Salvation is found in no one else, for there is no other name given under heaven by which we must be saved."*

What are we to do with this information? Do we truly believe it? When we come to understand that Jesus is the bridge to God and heaven and that we can affect a person's eternal destiny by keeping politely quiet, then we become motivated to evangelize.

The most unlikely of persons recognized this connection between faith and evangelism, even though he was not a believer. Charles Peace was a notorious British burglar and murderer who was finally caught, tried, and convicted for his crimes.

On September 25, 1879, an Anglican priest read the liturgy as the condemned man was led to the gallows for execution: "Those who die without Christ experience hell, which is the pain of forever dying without the release which death itself can bring."

Charlie Peace stopped and shouted at the priest, "Do you believe that? Do you believe that?"

Surprised by the unexpected outburst, the priest haltingly replied, "I...suppose I do."

"Well, I don't," said the convict, who was only minutes from death. "But if I did, I'd get down on my hands and knees and crawl all over Great Britain, even if it were paved with pieces of broken glass, if I could rescue one person from what you just told me."[9]

We, too, must come to that point where the consequences of keeping quiet make evangelism a real and important responsibility.

Reason #3: Because it works. The gospel of Jesus transforms people, and I mean more than the fact that they resist sin and start living godly lives. Christians have help and hope from God. They know what it means to experience joy despite life's difficulties. Through forgiveness, they are given relief from shame and guilt. They become part of a close and loving community of fellow believers who watch out for them, love them, and pray for them. They look forward to eternal life, a new and wonderful existence that comes after physical death on earth. They are promised help from the Holy Spirit of God who lives inside them.

So Christians experience the presence and power of God, which adds a whole new dimension to their lives. It is little wonder that true believers, God's abundantly satisfied customers, have good reason to share their experience with others. They want to connect others with a life that *works* and offer the hope that they have as Christians.

Paul saw the need

St. Paul became a passionate persuader for Christ. He did all that he could to sway unbelievers to become Christians. Here is a statement of his determination, in his own words:

> *Though I am free and belong to no one, I make myself a slave to everyone, to win as many as possible. To the Jews I became like a Jew, to win the Jews. To those under the law I became like one under the law (though I myself am not under the law), so as to win those under the law. To those not having the law I became like one not having the law (though I am not free from God's law but am under Christ's law), so as to win those not having the law. To the weak I became weak, to win the weak. I have become all things to all people so that by all possible means I might save some. I do all this for the sake of the gospel, that I may share in its blessings. (1 Corinthians 9:19-23)*

These are the words of a true believer willing to set aside his own preferences and comforts in order to evangelize others.

At what cost?

During the nineteenth century, the Dutch ruled a region of South America that is now called Suriname. A group of missionaries wanted to reach the people of a nearby island and tell them the good news about Jesus. Most of the islanders were slaves, and the plantation owners forbade the missionaries access out of fear of what would happen if the slaves became Christians. They imposed the rule that "only slaves may talk to slaves."[10]

An impossible situation? The missionaries came up with a way around the barrier. They sold themselves into slavery, becoming slaves themselves so that they could talk to the slaves. They worked at their sides, facing the same brutal treatment, a harsh tropical climate, hunger, and disease. They became slaves to share the good news of Jesus with people who might otherwise never hear that God loves every person and does not want anyone to die without hearing the message.

How to evangelize—the impossible made possible

We need to move from reasons to actions. Let's consider the steps we can take to put Jesus' instructions into actual deeds.

Believe. Belief is an action. We choose to believe that evangelism is good and that sharing the good news of Jesus is what we are supposed to do. This is not action motivated by guilt or fear. It is just belief. Let us tell God that we truly believe in Jesus, that we believe in evangelism, and that we believe we can be used by God to express a message of hope to others.

Care. This is an important next step for many of us. Many Christians believe with all their hearts, but that belief doesn't translate into genuine caring. When it comes to sharing the gospel, caring counts. Otherwise, I become a debater and an antagonist because of my sense of superiority and arrogance. As Christians, we need to humbly choose to care for others as Jesus cares.

Rebecca Oehrig is a young American missionary in Mozambique who recently wrote this letter describing her emotions at encountering people in terrible need:

> My country is dying. It is my country not by birth, nor by nationality, nor by choice, but it is a country that has chosen me and, despite my best efforts to remain somewhat aloof, has entwined itself in my heart. Today I weep for Mozambique. I weep for the sorrow that salts the air...the daily funerals...the broken homes. I weep for destitute widows and orphaned children. I weep for the still-breathing skeletons with hollow eyes that sit in a lonely wait for death. I weep for the hunger pangs, the bloated tummies, the oozing sores that eat at flesh that hangs like oversized clothing. I weep for the helplessness, the despair, the loneliness. I weep for myself because to me AIDS has names and faces. These are my friends.[11]

How can individuals who, deep down, don't truly care for people they have never met *learn* to care? We learn by getting to know people outside our comfortable world. Each of us needs to meet real people living real lives of difficulty without Jesus. If your church sponsors ministries to people in your community—whether food shelves, tutoring, youth programs, or whatever—get involved. Start out slowly if you're nervous, but get started. Don't stay cocooned in your own activities and busy life. Get to know people in need. God loves them, and you may be surprised at how quickly you care for them, too. Let us deeply care for someone beyond ourselves.

Pray. Christians pray for others. We pray for our families, our health, our jobs, our cars, and ourselves. Make another prayer list. Commit to praying for your neighbors, a great place to begin. Pray for the people in your city. Wonderful. Now pick a city or region or country somewhere else on the globe. Pray for the people who live there. Believe that prayer matters and makes a difference. Pray for a day, a week, a year, a decade. Pray for others to know Jesus.

Does prayer really matter? The people in a Phoenix church were challenged to randomly choose eighty names from the phone book and then pray for those individuals every day for ninety days. After the three months, the church members called one hundred and sixty people from the phone book—eighty who had been prayed for and eighty who had not. When asked if someone from the church could visit their homes only one of the eighty people who had not been prayed for said yes; forty-five of the people who had been prayed for welcomed a visit.[12]

So here's a tangible challenge for us. Make a list of eight people you know who are unbelievers, and pray for them every day for eight weeks. See what God does.

Talk. Talk about Jesus. Look for, seize, and create opportunities to talk about your Christian faith. Your words don't need to be a sermon—in fact, it would be much better if they weren't! Gently offer a word of encouragement, share an answer to prayer, quote a meaningful and timely line from the Bible, briefly discuss an encounter with God, or lend a book. "Wait a minute!" you protest, "Isn't there a law that forbids me from talking about religion?" Actually, there is no such law, and people talk about their faith all the time. A survey by the Barna Research Group reports that more than ninety million adults talk about spiritual issues every week.[13] As a Christian, try talking less about politics and more about Jesus!

Invite. Bring people you care about to church. By far, the top reason anyone comes to any church for the first time is because a good friend, respected co-worker, or loving family member invites him or her. Consider people you know with whom you could share a positive church experience. Now, stop thinking and invite them! Need a specific goal? Invite at least twelve people to church or a church event in the next twelve months. You needn't apply pressure or lay on the guilt. Just ask. The answer you receive may surprise you.

Give. Money is just one element of evangelism, but it's an important and powerful way to send missionaries where you can't easily go. Every true Christian should regularly and generously give financial support to evangelism around the world. What is evangelism but the bringing of hope and help to people in great need?

I'm an advocate of Christians supporting their local church because, as a pastor, I think about the reality of paying the church mortgage, meeting staff payroll, and providing resources to many valuable, on-site ministry areas. But I am even more convinced that every follower of Jesus should sacrificially give to support the global advance of the gospel. Missions is the greatest cause in the world. Don't leave it to everyone else. Give to missions.

Think about bottled water. It costs more than gasoline. Americans spend over $10 billion per year on Evian, Poland Springs, La Croix, and other brands of water; yet blind tests have shown that there is no distinguishable difference in the purity or taste of bottled water over tap water.[14] At the same time, millions of people around the world are dying from drinking unclean water that could be purified through filtration systems. I'm not trying to talk anyone out of a bottle of water, but I would like to convince every Christian to think about how much money we spend on beverages and to give at least as much and more to touch the lives of others in Jesus' name.

Go. Become a missionary. Your journey may be to the other side of the world for a lifetime or it may be across the street to meet a new neighbor. It may be to translate the Bible into a now-unwritten language or to build a house for a poor family in Guatemala. It may be as a church planter in Venice or as a computer programmer in Vietnam. Perhaps you will consider a career in missions. Or maybe you'll take a short-term adventure with your church to see what God is doing and experience how even a brief missions trip can open your heart to the people who had, until now, seemed so far away. The first step in going is to ask God where to go and what to do.

Take the challenge seriously

You are a Christian. Christians care enough to share the very best. Frankly, we cannot call ourselves Christians if we do not evangelize. Evangelism is what we do—not just once (to get it over with!), not by begrudgingly giving a dollar or two, but as a way of life.

On March 15, 2004, I was in Atlanta to speak to Southern Baptist church leaders. The conference was interrupted by the devastating announcement that five Southern Baptist missionaries had been killed in Iraq. One of them was Karen Watson. I later learned that she had written a letter to the pastors of her home church to be opened and read in case of her death.

Near the end of her letter are words of instruction that could be guiding principles for Christians who have given their hearts and minds to the great job of evangelism:

> *Care more than some think is wise.*
> *Risk more than some think is safe.*
> *Dream more than some think is practical.*
> *Expect more than some think is possible.*[15]

37

Part Two:
The Christian Mind...
Imitating the Mind of Christ

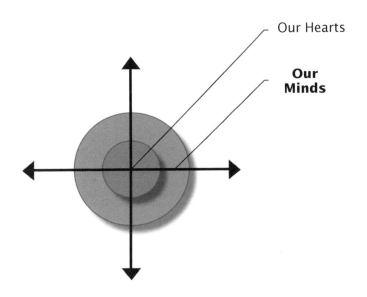

Our Hearts

Our Minds

Chapter Four

Managing Money Like God is Going to Ask

Biographies do more than tell the story of a person's life—they reveal an individual's values and character. The writers of biographies may cite newspaper articles, interviews, letters, and speeches to find that deep, inner self, but some would say we can learn more from a person's checkbook than from a diary.

Most of us will not have our biographies published—a fact that we may embrace with a great sense of relief—but we do have checkbooks, credit card statements, and income tax returns. These items tell much about the kind of people we are. The evidence is right there. As Christians, we want our finances to reflect our faith because the way we manage money is one of the best indicators of our relationship with Jesus.

Money was on Jesus' mind

Why was money so important to Jesus? Sixteen of Jesus' thirty-eight parables are about money and possessions. One out of ten verses in the New Testament Gospels deals with money. One

41

Bible counter says that in the entire Bible there are fewer than five hundred verses on prayer, fewer than five hundred verses on faith, and more than two thousand verses about money and possessions.[16] Apparently, money has something important to do with our faith and our closeness with God.

We who are Christians want to reflect Jesus Christ in every part of our lives—including finances. But we're a diverse group, and that makes it difficult to talk about money. Some have millions of dollars, houses that are paid off, retirement accounts, stock holdings, and a vast collection of expensive possessions. Others can barely make the rent payment. Some are homeless and don't know where their next meal will be found. Some have long-term jobs and a sense of great security. Others are teetering on the verge of unemployment. Still others are unemployed. Some people are blessed with the skill of managing money; others have little wisdom in handling their income. Some are intuitively generous. Others desire to hang onto their wealth, whatever its size, for security. But if we are Christians, we should want to act like Jesus Christ, regardless of our individual circumstances.

Let's look at New Testament teachings about how Christians handle money and—with open hearts—ask God to teach us how to handle money like followers of Jesus.

Prepare by praying

If you desire to follow Jesus' teachings in this area, start the process by briefly and privately praying to God.

Thank God for all that God has given to you.

Whatever you have is a blessing. So give God your gratitude!

Tell God your current financial situation.

You know what challenges you face. Share them openly with God.

Ask God for wisdom about how to manage money.

As Christians, we have the Holy Spirit as a financial advisor. Ask God to teach you, through the Holy Spirit, what you need to know.

Promise God that you will try to handle money like a Christian.

Once you ask for help, be prepared to do what needs to be done. Listen to God.

Look at the biblical principles

Consider how our actions and attitude can reflect Christ's by starting with the Bible. The following principles show ways to act like a Christian when it comes to possessions. How do they apply to your current financial situation?

Principle #1: Choose God over money. Jesus made a direct and irrefutable statement in Luke 16:13: *"No one can serve two masters. Either you will hate the one and love the other, or you will be devoted to the one and despise the other. You cannot serve both God and Money."* According to Jesus, it's a choice between two deities: God and Money.

Notice that the translators capitalized the word money. That accurately and timelessly reflects society's temptation to idolize money as a god. We are under constant pressure to choose whether our money will turn into Money. The decisions we make about where we work, how we spend our time, and how we spend our income are all determined by our attitude regarding its importance in our lives.

As Christians we want to say, "I choose God. God is more important to me than money or anything else." But saying that gets more difficult when we're faced with real, day-to-day decisions. We live in a culture where money means almost everything. People live for it. They define their self-worth and status by how much they can accumulate. In this context, it can be a surprisingly difficult struggle to stay a balanced Christian.

Ready for a test? Here are some practical life applications. What would you choose?

1. You have a choice between marrying a rich unbeliever and a poor Christian. Whom would you select? (Picking the rich unbeliever and converting him or her is not an option!)

2. Would you rather your son or daughter marry a rich unbeliever or a poor Christian?

3. Would you rather read the Bible or a money magazine?

4. If someone gave you a thousand dollars, would you save it, spend it, or give it to the poor in the name of Jesus Christ?

These questions are not meant to heap guilt on you. They are only a brief evaluation to help you honestly determine your priorities. Even when we know better, it's not always easy to maintain a healthy, Christian perspective on money. In our culture, the temptation to value money more highly than we should is relentless. The values of our world saturate the TV we watch, the books we read, the conversations we have, and—inevitably—our attitudes.

Managing money as a Christian doesn't mean that we shouldn't enjoy life or money. I have an item on my current prayer list that reminds me to "enjoy God's blessings." If God has given us resources, we should enjoy them. We don't need to feel guilty about the provision of good meals, warm beds, and a car that starts in the wintertime. We should be grateful for those things! However, we should always see money and possessions in terms of God, and we should always make it clear that we choose God first. Then "letting go" can result in changes in the way we live our lives.

Principle #2: Plan ahead. God is a planner. God has a plan for each of our lives. God planned creation. God planned salvation. God expressed divine plans through prophecy. Planning is God-like, and an activity that we should pursue.

Planning ahead means that we think before we act, pray before we commit, and consider the consequences before we make decisions. Jesus asked his listeners to consider a realistic scenario that illustrated this concept. *"Suppose one of you wants to build a tower. Won't you first sit down and estimate the cost to see if you have enough money to complete it? For if you lay the foundation and are not able to finish it, everyone who sees it will ridicule you, saying, 'This person began to build and wasn't able to finish'"* (Luke 14:28-30).

Because most of us are not planning to build towers any time soon, I'll paraphrase Jesus' words for our generation. Thinking about building a house? Make sure you have enough money before you sign the contract. Want to buy or lease a car? Be sure you can make the payment. Considering a vacation that you will charge to your credit card? Make certain that you can pay the charges when the statement comes. Setting up a new business? Plan for the year or more when the company will not be profitable. As Christians, let us think before we spend, plan ahead, have a budget, schedule our contributions, plan our retirement, prepare for an emergency, and so on. Christians plan.

Understand that planning and trusting are not contradictory. You may have heard a well-intentioned person say, "Don't plan anything. When you get there, God will meet you, and everything will work out just fine. It's arrogant to plan ahead." But we can trust God in both the planning *and* the fulfillment of plans, always recognizing that our plans are not guarantees. Things can change. Plans can go right or wrong, and God *will* be there for us, regardless. For committed Christians, trusting and planning are connected like faith and good works.

Principle #3: Invest wisely. Wise investing is one of the points of a famous parable in Matthew 25. Jesus' story is about a wealthy boss who was headed out of town on a long trip. Before he left, he set up three trust funds to be managed by three of his employees. The first trust fund had five bags of gold, the second contained two, and the third had one.[17] He instructed each employee to care for his money.

In the parable, the boss returned home after his journey and gathered his three employees together for a report. Employee number one announced, "I doubled your money from five to ten bags of gold." The boss was delighted. The second employee crowed, "I doubled your money from two to four bags of gold." Again, the boss was pleased. The third employee stepped forward. *"I was afraid and went out and hid your gold in the ground. See, here is what belongs to you."* He had nothing to offer except exactly what had been given to him to manage.

The employer showered the first two investors with praise. He said, *"Well done, good and faithful servant! You have been faithful with a few things; I will put you in charge of many things. Come and share your master's happiness!"* But he was deeply disappointed with the third employee and reproached him sternly: *"You should have put my money on deposit with the bankers, so that when I returned I would have received it back with interest."* The third employee hadn't even done the minimum! His boss took the trust fund away and turned it over to employee number one (an action, by the way, that made good financial sense). The third employee had demonstrated that he was lousy at investing and managing the assets that he had been blessed with.

What we have here is not a mini-course on Christian economics but a lesson from Jesus that we should be wise with cash and possessions because they belong to God. Our goods are in trust funds that we manage until God eventually calls us to account. How might Jesus' message translate into twenty-first century English? Here are a few ideas:

Save money. Don't spend everything you get. You can't invest wisely if you don't have something to invest.

A financial advisor I know sometimes works with people who are in the midst of catastrophic financial circumstances and deeply in debt. They come to him, in desperation, for help. He listens, looks at all of the numbers and says, "The first thing you need to do is open a savings account."

Almost always, the response is, "Haven't you been listening? I'm telling you I don't *have* any money!" Still, the advisor insists that they open the account and explains why. People who save money have a transformed view of the rest of their money. In desperate times, a systemic change is needed. If they don't make a change, they will never get out of debt.

So save. Even if you are in debt, even if it seems that you don't have enough to live on, even if you already have more money than you need—save. Save instead of going into debt. Save for retirement. Save in order to generously give. Perhaps you can only manage to put away one cent per day for a total of $3.65 a year. Do it! Notice that the main difference in Jesus' parable was not the amount earned but how the talents were handled. Get in the habit of saving. Show God you are a good manager, and see if God will entrust you with more.

Learn how money works. Some of us grew up in families where our parents didn't have an inkling of how to handle money. As a result, we don't have much of an idea either. We can learn.

In Jesus' parable the boss complained that, at the very least, the third employee could have deposited the talent in a bank and received interest. But there is no hint that the employee did even basic research into wise investment options. He could have asked the other employees for advice. He could have asked a banker for help. He could have learned better ways to invest to earn his boss's trust.

We, too, can take advantage of the resources around us. Our world is financially complex, and we should know something about modern money management in order to survive. Instead, some of us don't take advantage of employer's matching contributions to retirement plans; we don't ask others for financial advice; we don't talk to a banker. Some of us take the easy but unwise course of burying our heads and cash in the sand.

As Christians, we may not become financial investment geniuses, but we ought to know the basics. We can take a money management course at a church or at a school. We can read a book. We can talk to experts. We can learn how to wisely invest the resources God has entrusted to us.

Give regularly. Giving is what Christians do. It's one sure sign that someone is faithfully following Jesus Christ. It's an essential quality of Christian behavior. One reason we plan and invest is so that we can more generously give it away!

St. Paul set up a system for first century Christians who gathered for worship and teaching. He wrote, *"Now about the collection for the Lord's people: Do what I told the Galatian churches to do. On the first day of every week, each one of you should set aside a sum of money in keeping with your income, saving it up, so that when I come no collections will have to be made"* (1 Corinthians 16:1-2).

The church members in Corinth pooled their offerings, and Paul, as their agent, transported and distributed that money to poor Christians in Jerusalem. They set a precedent that has been followed by Christians for two thousand years—the taking of offerings when Christians gather. These contributions can then be channeled to the poor, charities, church ministries, missions, and needy individuals. I believe that the clear biblical teaching here is that Christians give together through the church, but that isn't the primary point. Christians give because Jesus gave, because we are grateful, because we want to advance the cause of Jesus, and because God asks us to give. We give to the poor. We give to the church. We give to help others. We give whether we get a tax deduction or not. We give whether we are thanked or not. Christians give.

We should give significantly, sacrificially, consistently, and proportionately. What we give should grow proportionately with the resources God provides. Somebody who makes $10,000 a year will probably give a smaller amount than somebody who earns $50,000 or $100,000 a year. The main point is not the amount; rather it is the discipline, the pattern. If you are a Christian, giving should be a regular part of your life.

If you don't currently give, get started! As with savings, you can start small and build the habit. Put a penny in. Put a dollar in. Give every week. Don't let the offering plate or basket pass you by! Grow the habit, and deal with the amount later. You will be glad. You will be blessed. You will be acting like a Christian.

And don't stop there. Put a dollar in the hand of a poor person every week. Be consistent in demonstrating Christ's generosity. Just get into the habit. Find a piggy bank, wallet, or coin purse, and use it in creative ways to bless others. Fill the piggy bank, and give it to someone who needs some cash. Regularly put small amounts of money into the wallet. When it is full, put it into the church offering. Load up the coin purse and prepare to hand it to the next homeless person you see. Your goal as a blessed Christian is not to "pig-out" on the money God has entrusted to you. Instead, you can grow as a follower of Jesus by giving. You will discover the joy and blessing that he intended when he instructed us to give. You'll experience the trust that God places in those who are Christians and generous. Be a giver.

Provide for your family. This is a primary New Testament teaching. *"Anyone who does not provide for their relatives, and especially for their own household, has denied the faith and is worse than an unbeliever"* (1 Timothy 5:8).

Over the years, I've been impressed by the way Christians care unselfishly for their family members. Their generosity and concern don't stop with children or mothers and fathers but extend to brothers, sisters, aunts, uncles, cousins, nephews, and nieces! We aren't called to enable people to continue with dysfunctional behavior, but we should always be open and caring enough to do everything we can to provide what is most needed: housing, financial gifts, help with jobs, tuition, clothing, cars, and more.

There are other, practical ways we can use money to provide for our families:

- *Get a will.* If you have financial resources and don't have a will, then make it a priority to get one—now! Before finishing this book! If you don't have a will, the government will decide what happens to your money and possessions. It will be the government's role to decide how your family will be provided for. Don't shirk your Christian responsibility and hand over decisions to the government.

- *Buy life insurance,* especially if your family depends on your income. Make sure that they will be provided for when you die.

- *Limit debt.* Debt is tough on families. It steals the future, limits options, and reduces resources. We rationalize debt, saying, "I'm taking my family on a vacation they'll never forget. I'm buying them clothes, toys, and the latest electronic gadgets because I love them and want to make them happy." But if these things force you into debt, choose instead to give them the joy of debt-free living. We need Christian discipline to live modestly.

Money can tell the story of your life

Your biography is being written—in your checkbook, your credit card statements, your income tax returns, and your everyday dealings with money. May your friends now and your great-great grandchildren someday describe you as the kind of Christian who chose God over cash, the kind of Christian who managed money like God is going to ask.

Chapter Five

Setting Sexual Boundaries

If ever there was an opportunity to demonstrate what it means to be distinctively Christian, it is in the area of sexual behavior in the twenty-first century.

The distinction between godly and ungodly sexual behavior has been around since the Garden of Eden, where God first introduced sex. Each new generation must deal with its particular culture and the temptations that it faces. In our culture today, there is an emphasis on sex that is generally not positive. Rather than representations of loving sex between committed and faithful husbands and wives, we see casual promiscuity, degradation of women, sexualization of children, and disturbing perversions. While none of these issues is new to our world, today they are pervasive. In addition, they are uniquely accessible.

We live in a society of unique temptation. The previous generation had access to pornography but not so easily and anonymously through the Internet. Other generations had promiscuity, but it was not promoted to mass audiences in prime time television programs. Immorality—behavior that God would consider outside his perfect plan for human beings—surrounds us and may even seem, at times, to be engulfing us.

I've read the surveys and agree that the statistics about modern sexual attitudes and behavior can be discouraging. Christians who read the news or who are confronted with sexual content in films, advertising, television, and music can't help but wonder about the state of sexual attitudes in our world. Is purity possible anymore? Is it hopelessly out of date?

Instead of focusing on disheartening statistics and the obvious consequences of immorality in our world—everything from disappointment to depression to disease to divorce—let's focus on the healthy Christian's perspective on sex. After all, the reason we behave like Christians is not to avoid herpes but to honor God.

God's great idea: sex

Here's the reality: sex is good. When we are attracted to someone of the opposite sex, it is because God designed us that way. When sex feels good, it is because God thought up those feelings. In fact, sex is one of the ways we live for God. Our sexuality is not separate from our Christian life. When we think about sex, it should drive us back to thinking about God. How we think of our sexuality—and how we practice it—is one way of honoring God.

Let's go back to the beginning, when two separate human sexes (and sexuality) first made their appearance. The powerful distinction between male and female and all the sexual wonder that surrounds it is part of the creation story.

> *Then the* Lord *God made a woman from the rib he had taken out of the man, and he brought her to the man. The man said, "This is now bone of my bones and flesh of my flesh; she shall be called 'woman,' for she was taken out of man." For this reason a man will leave his father and mother and be united to his wife, and they will become one flesh. The man and his wife were both naked, and they felt no shame.* (Genesis 2:22-25)

Try to imagine the wonder and splendor of Adam and Eve seeing each other for the first time. They were obviously very much alike—both thoroughly and completely human—and they were very different. Their bodies were naked, beautiful, attractive, sensual, and designed to come together. The whole plan was magnificent and powerful. They felt no shame or embarrassment, just sheer joy. And God was delighted.

> *So God created human beings in his own image, in the image of God he created them; male and female he created them... God saw all that he had made, and it was very good.* (Genesis 1:27, 31)

Why is sex so important?

Since that moment of creation, sexuality has been one of the premiere, defining features of human beings. Yes, humans are complex. We define ourselves by many factors, including language, race, nationality, and age, but gender is at the top of the list. The Bible even refers to gender in heaven. The gender you are now is what you will be throughout eternity in heaven.[18] Whether we are babies in the nursery, aged in the nursing home, single, married, celibate, or sexually active, our sex is an integral part of our identity. It is part of who God created us to be. That is why our sexual roles and practices are important and why sexual abuse is so damaging.

Too often we equate sex with the physical union of two bodies, but it is much more than that. It's the way we dress. It's the pitch of our voices. It's the way we walk. It is the way we think. How we behave sexually is woven into all of life and is at the core of how we act like Christians.

Because sexuality is so important, Christians should not relegate it to a separate silo in our lives. Frankly, that temptation is a problem for many people and deeply affects their spiritual development. There are Christians who say, "Jesus Christ is my Savior. He is my Lord. I love him. I want to do everything that he wants me to do and be his follower whether it's how I speak, handle money, pray, or serve others—except for sex." It is as if there is one room in their lives that has a locked door to keep God out. But, it doesn't work that way. God knows about every area that we try to exclude. No matter what we rationalize and cover up, God says that our sexuality and our Christianity are wired together.

God's great protection: boundaries

Because our God-given sexuality is so powerful, God gave boundaries to protect us from dangers, something he has graciously done in many arenas of life. Life itself is a powerful gift, so God has placed boundaries against assault and murder. God has given us property and possessions but with the boundary against theft. God has given us truth, a marvelous gift protected by a boundary against lying.

To make clear some of God's sexual boundaries for humans, God gave a list of rules to the Israelites that appear in the Old Testament book of Leviticus:

> *No one is to approach any close relative to have sexual relations. I am the LORD. Do not dishonor your father by having sexual relations with your mother. She is your mother; do not have relations with her. Do not have sexual relations with your father's wife; that would dishonor your father. Do not have sexual relations with your sister, either your father's daughter or your mother's daughter, whether she was born in the same home or elsewhere.* (Leviticus 18:6-9)

The list goes on and the list is long. With a few exceptions, the vast majority of modern Americans would agree to live within these common sense boundaries. Most of these rules are codified in our modern criminal laws.

With or without those laws, almost all people have their own set of personal boundaries. Who sets those boundaries—us or God? As Christians, we believe in the God who created us and our sexuality, and we also believe that God sets boundaries for our good and his honor. The Bible helps us to know the mind of God in this area.

Flee from sexual immorality. All other sins people commit are outside their bodies, but those who sin sexually sin against their own bodies. Do you not know that your bodies are temples of the Holy Spirit, who is in you, whom you have received from God? You are not your own; you were bought at a price. Therefore honor God with your bodies. (1 Corinthians 6:18-20)

Again and again, the Bible reminds us that God has a special view of sexuality. It challenges us to pull away from the pervasive cultural view of sex as casual or crude, and instead look at it through the eyes of God.

It is God's will that you should be sanctified: that you should avoid sexual immorality; that each of you should learn to control your own body in a way that is holy and honorable, not in passionate lust like the pagans, who do not know God. (1 Thessalonians 4:3-5)

Clearly, Christians are to be different when it comes to this wonderful, God-given part of their lives.

What's your motivation?

To someone who is not a Christian, I suggest enjoying the gift of sex because, as God made clear, it is "very good." But I also suggest staying within the sexual boundaries God has given. Even if an individual's focus is on how to best care for himself or herself, living within God's design for sex is wise and good. God's boundaries protect people.

However, if you are a Christian, your motivation is very different. We are God-centered. We have a relationship with Jesus Christ and have declared allegiance to him as the Lord of our lives, including our sexual lives. Our goal is to please him. That means that in everything, we choose to honor him and make him look good, even when it is difficult. We choose to act like Christians in our sexual choices and behavior.

How does a Christian act?

Acting like a Christian will depend on our situation.

For someone who is single, it means abstaining from sexual intimacy until marriage. It means choosing not to live together before marriage. It means resisting the temptation to rationalize immoral sexual behavior even if others around you—your peers, your friends, and characters you see in films and television programs—seem to condone it and call it normal and healthy.

For someone who is married, it means faithfulness—even if you are attracted to someone else. It means giving yourself sexually to your husband or wife more for their satisfaction than your own satisfaction. It means that sex is an expression of intimacy rather than a pathway to find intimacy.

For all of us, regardless of age or marital status, it means that we worship God with our bodies and with our sexual activities and that we consciously avoid immorality in what we view, what we say, and how we act.

At stake is the reputation of Jesus. When certain members of a sports team are involved in sexual misconduct, the whole team looks bad. When a politician behaves immorally, it reflects poorly on the image of the whole country. And when someone who professes to be a Christian continues sexual practices that are outside of God's boundaries, it makes Jesus Christ look bad. As Christians, we want to make Jesus look good!

On living a sexually pure life: practical advice

There are hundreds of practical ways for us to increase our likelihood of staying within the sexual boundaries God has set up for us.

Be careful what you drink. Researchers report overwhelming connections between alcohol consumption and immoral sex.[19] When teenagers lose their virginity to a casual friend, when a woman becomes the victim of a date rape, or when an individual commits adultery with a co-worker, chances are very high that alcohol or drugs were involved. If you want to act like a Christian in sex, be careful what you drink. The Bible advises us:

> *Be very careful, then, how you live—not as unwise but as wise, making the most of every opportunity, because the days are evil. Therefore do not be foolish, but understand what the Lord's will is. Do not get drunk on wine, which leads to debauchery. Instead, be filled with the Spirit.* (Ephesians 5:15-18)

Abstain from pornography. Easy access to pornography has become a curse of our generation. Pornography is the crack cocaine of sexual addictions. While there are many issues that should make us avoid pornography, one big reason is that viewing these images is essentially selfish. Pornography doesn't promote the intimacy that sex is designed to be all about. It makes sex all about "me" and quick gratification, no matter who is being exploited. No one is exempt from this temptation, men or women, so set your standards ahead of time, and don't give into the appeal of easy access. Perhaps pornography is consuming more and more hours of your week and your thoughts. This is my urgent advice, especially to Christian men who are among the one-third of Americans accessing Internet pornography and are now addicted.[20] Get help. Tell a friend. Talk to your wife. See a counselor. Join a support group.

If you are not yet addicted but are tempted or are viewing pornography, buy a computer filter. Put your computer in a public place at home. Switch to an Internet service provider that restricts access. Although it seems extreme, get rid of your computer if you must.

Dress modestly. Think through the sexual implications of the clothes you buy and the cosmetics you wear. Certainly you can be attractive and celebrate your physical beauty, but don't be provocative. Don't intentionally attract sexual attention or purposely trigger lust. When others say you are "hot" or your outfit is "sexy," don't take it as a great compliment. Instead, accept it as an indicator that it may be time to reconsider your selection of clothing. If you're a Christian, your modesty is a reflection of Jesus.

When in doubt, ask the opinion of someone of the opposite gender or wear something else. The question of what to wear is not a new issue. 1 Timothy 2:9-10 states, *"I also want the women to dress modestly, with decency and propriety...with good deeds, appropriate for women who profess to worship God"* (1 Timothy 2:9-10). This instruction is not meant to hamper or reduce individuality. It is a practical boundary that helps maintain a closer relationship with God and honor him rather than yourself.

Think clean. Thoughts aren't visible on the outside, but they are no less important from God's perspective than modest clothing. If you are troubled by inappropriate sexual thoughts—thoughts that objectify other people, that demean your marriage, or that interfere with your closeness with God, choose to make a change. Philippians 4:8 gives us a goal statement and a command: *"Whatever is true, whatever is noble, whatever is right, whatever is pure, whatever is lovely, whatever is admirable—if anything is excellent or praiseworthy—think about such things."* If you desire a real change in your thinking you will need to actively pursue different thoughts. You may not be able to accomplish this feat on your own, but God can give you the power you need to overhaul your mind!

Set sexual limits in advance. Most of us aren't good at deciding sexual boundaries in the heat of passion or in the face of temptation. Ask God to help you set sexual limits in advance—before going to the prom, before the business trip to Las Vegas, before going to a party, before signing up for cable TV. If somebody else is involved, set the limits together. Have a very frank discussion and decide what the boundaries are going to be. Write them down. Be specific, and don't play word games to rationalize immoral behavior by saying that intimate sexual activities are not really sex. Ask for God's help to stay well within the limits.

Keep speech moral. What we say is a clear window into the true state of our souls and an expression of our faith. Don't speak obscenities. Don't repeat immoral jokes. Don't turn God's good sex into crude immorality. There's even a verse that commands Christians to guard the way we talk about sex.

> *But among you there must not be even a hint of sexual immorality, or of any kind of impurity, or of greed, because these are improper for the Lord's people. Nor should there be obscenity, foolish talk or coarse joking, which are out of place.* (Ephesians 5:3-4)

Start over. If your sexual behavior has been less than Christian, you can start over. You wanted to be a virgin when you married, and now you're not. You never wanted to see pornography, and now you are addicted. You hated the idea of unfaithfulness, but now you're having an affair. You promised God you'd never live with someone before marriage, but you've already moved in.

Tell God you were wrong. Pour out your heart, and tell God you are sorry. God will forgive you and offer a fresh opportunity to act like a Christian in the area of sex. If you've already started over before and messed up—whether one or many times—start again. If you've started over a hundred times and feel like a failure, go to God, ask for help, and start all over again.

Weigh the benefits

I know a man who grew up in a non-Christian religion. When he went off to college in the Midwest, he had never met a Christian in his life.

On the first day of school, he saw an attractive young woman sitting, next to an empty seat, so he sat down and introduced himself to her. She told him her name and explained that she was a born-again Christian. He didn't know what she meant or why she would say such a thing. It was like meeting someone for the first time who promptly announced that she was allergic to asparagus.

He pursued her, and they became friends. Months later, he came to her room to study and while they were studying, he came close and pushed her down on the bed. She immediately reacted, pushed him away, and told him off in words that left no room for misunderstanding. She made her relational and sexual boundaries clear.

He told her that she totally misunderstood what had happened. He didn't mean anything sexual at all. He was stunned and offended that she would think ill of him. He flat out lied.

The young woman did something that took him completely by surprise. She believed him. She apologized for accusing him of sexual advances that he said he did not intend and asked for his forgiveness.

He left her room and walked alone down the hall. Something struck him that had never entered his thoughts before that moment. For the first time in his life, he fully realized that he had done something wrong. His intentions *had* been sinful, and he knew it. This young man was totally taken aback by the stunning righteousness and purity of the woman he had just deceived.

The experience became a pivotal moment in his life. By the example and influence of that eighteen-year-old young woman, he became a Christian. He graduated from the university, went on to law school, and became the professor of law at one of the largest universities in America. Today, he is a pastor. And he married that righteous young woman.

That college freshman lived out all that it means to act like a Christian when it comes to sexual attitudes and behavior. If she could do it, so can we.

Chapter Six

Making Important Decisions

Rick Warren opens his best selling book, *The Purpose Driven Life*, with this startling statement: "It's not about you."[21]

Believing this concept to be true is a distinguishing mark of the Christian. Not everything in life is about us. The world does not revolve around us—our desires, our needs, and our lives. It centers on God. What is good for God is good for us. If God is happy, we are happy. Holding this point of view naturally results in changed behavior. If God wants us to do something, we do it. And if God says, "Don't," we don't. The apostle Paul sums it up in Romans 12:2: *"Do not conform to the pattern of this world, but be transformed by the renewing of your mind. Then you will be able to test and approve what God's will is—his good, pleasing and perfect will."*

This way of thinking runs contrary to the daily messages of our culture, which tell us to "Watch out for Number One. Do what you want, get what you want, and enjoy life!" Christians say, "That's totally wrong. There's so much more. God is good. Pleasing God is our most important task." We believe that God wants what's best for us. It's at the center of God's heart. And because God's will for our lives is perfect, we put God first.

Whom do you most want to please? Your answer to that question will determine how you make decisions.

What are *your* concerns?

A survey in the congregation I serve asked people about their deepest concerns and the decisions they faced. "If you could ask God about his will for your life, what would you ask?" The answers came back in these general categories: purpose in life; marriage; career; missing God's will; and what to do after difficulty or defeat.

"Should I marry the person I'm dating?"

"Should I quit my job, go back to school, and start a new career?"

"I married the wrong person. Should I get a divorce and find someone else?"

"Should I sell my house and car and get out of debt?"

The Christians we polled wanted to understand God's will and apply it to their decision-making. So how do we do it?

Love God

One Christian theologian said that Christians should love God and then do as they please. On first glance that seems troublesome. But look at what he's saying. If we love and serve God, then—under that umbrella—our decisions will be good ones. Jesus said, *"Love the Lord your God with all your heart and with all your soul and with all your mind and with all your strength"* (Mark 12:30). Anyone who loves God that passionately can do whatever she wants. Too often, we put more energy into making a decision than into loving God. We need to love God more.

Check the Bible

The Bible contains practical advice. If the Bible says that something is wrong, don't do it. If it is silent on the subject, don't sweat it. Are you thinking about moving in with the person you've been dating? Don't do it. The Bible advises against premarital sex. Do you want to marry someone who is not a Christian? Whoa. The Bible is very clear that Christians should marry other Christians.

Suppose that the major decision you're facing is choosing the color of car you should buy. You've read the Bible all the way through looking for guidance and help in this matter, and you have concluded that God has no color preference. I do—red—but God, apparently, doesn't. So pick any color you want! The Bible doesn't tell us which job to take, where we should invest our money, or whether we should go out for lacrosse or football. But it does tell us that we should work honestly, invest wisely, and play fairly. Read the Bible if you want solid guidelines for your decisions.

Pray for wisdom

When the Bible is direct in its instructions, we don't need to pray about it. If you've been agonizing over a decision about whether or not to rob a bank, save your time. Don't ask God which bank. Just don't do it. God has been clear, and it is simply not a subject for prayer. Do what the Bible tells you.

But what if you're struggling in those gray areas of uncertainty where the choice could go either way? As a Christian who thoroughly loves God, you want to get this right. So pray and ask for wisdom. James 1:5 tells us: *"If any of you lacks wisdom, you should ask God, who gives generously to all without finding fault, and it will be given to you."* Wisdom is the application of knowledge and information. It is a gift from God given to every Christian who asks for it.

Imagine trying to decide whether to rent this apartment or another one. "God," you pray, "I've checked out all these apartments. I've compared all the rent. I want to live in the right place. I want to have the right relationships. God, show me which apartment to rent." Let me suggest a totally different prayer: "God, give to me the wisdom to figure this out and do the best thing." Pray, as we have been instructed in the New

Testament, for the wisdom that you need from God in order to make a good decision.

Ask for advice

None of us is smart enough or experienced enough to make totally independent decisions. The sage of Proverbs 15:22 says, *"Plans fail for lack of counsel, but with many advisers they succeed."* That's a principle, of course, not a guarantee. If you have fourteen advisers who are jerks, your plan probably *won't* succeed. But it's a good principle that you've probably experienced yourself: things go better when you get good counsel from wise advisors.

I like to get advice from others. Often, I turn to my wife, Charleen, for advice on issues big and small. I talk to co-workers. I seek the insight of the elders at the church I serve. I turn to professionals in the community. Input from multiple trusted sources is good. It gives me different perspectives. I seek counsel in order to have information so that a wise decision can be made, recognizing that not everyone's counsel is equal. I've learned that some people give terrible advice. That is one of the advantages of experience in life. Eventually we learn to select people who will give helpful advice.

The best combination is to get counsel from somebody who is both competent and godly. I must be honest and say that some friends are truly godly—but incompetent. They love God but give terrible advice. Don't expect your grace-filled best friend to know about 401(k)s! Likewise, there are some ungodly professionals who give very good advice on their topic of expertise. Get advice on the apartment rental from the apartment expert, but when you need spiritual counsel, go to the godly friend or pastor.

Take responsibility

Understand that getting counsel from others does not relieve us of responsibility. Advice is advice. Counsel is counsel. But each of us is responsible for the decisions that we make. None of us ought to fall back on, "Yeah, but he said—," or "She told me that I should—." We are still ultimately responsible for our own choices.

Just decide

It's time to choose. You've followed all of the other directives. You've made a list of pros and cons. You've thought it over. Just choose.

When making choices, we rarely have all the facts we need for a good decision. Imagine having all information at our disposal. Decisions would be easy. But we rarely have that luxury. New Testament Christians—authors of the Bible, people who were close to God—made decisions with the same limitations. Let's look at their methods.

In Acts 15:28, read the story about a council of church leaders meeting in Jerusalem to decide how non-Jews can become Christians. It was one of the most important theological decisions ever made in the history of Christianity. Acts 15:28 says, *"It seemed good to the Holy Spirit and to us not to burden you with anything beyond the following requirements."* So they made this major decision because it seemed like a good idea!

In Acts 19:21 more of Paul's decision-making process is recorded: *"After all this had happened, Paul decided to go to Jerusalem, passing through Macedonia and Achaia. 'After I have been there,' he said, 'I must visit Rome also.'"* He didn't have a written message from God; he just decided.

His travels and itinerary are recorded in Acts 20:2-3: *"He traveled through that area, speaking many words of encouragement to the people, and finally arrived in Greece, where he stayed three months. Because the Jews had plotted against him just as he was about to sail for Syria, he decided to go back through Macedonia."* He just decided. Because there was opposition, he changed his itinerary.

Read Acts 20:16. *"Paul had decided to sail past Ephesus to avoid spending time in the province of Asia, for he was in a hurry to reach Jerusalem, if possible, by the day of Pentecost."* So this is the process that is recorded in the New Testament. He looked at his calendar and said, logically, "If I'm going to make it there in time, I'd better go another way."

Now look at 1 Thessalonians 3:1. Paul writes, *"So when we could stand it no longer, we thought it best to be left by ourselves in Athens."* The "we" here is Paul and his colleague Silas. Read the next line, and you'll discover that they left Timothy behind.

Talk about making a major decision! Paul's choice affected the whole direction of Timothy's life. In essence his decision meant, "Sorry, Timothy. You're no longer on the team. I'm sending you in a different direction." And how did he make that choice? He "thought it best." It seemed like a good idea. (See 2 Corinthians 8:10.)

So even when Paul made a critical decision, there wasn't lightning from heaven. There was no sudden certainty that this was God's absolute and clear direction. You won't find any statements in the Bible about him having "peace of heart." He loved God, checked Scripture, asked for wisdom, and sought counsel. Then, based on the best information he had at the time, he made his choice.

Making peace with our decisions

Did the heroes of the Old and New Testaments always get their choices right? How about Christians today? The answer depends on what you mean by "right." If you mean, "Everything turned out happy and pleasant," then, no, it is obvious that decisions made by people of faith don't always turn out that way.

For Christians, the point isn't, "How did the decision turn out?" but, "How did I make that decision?" Suppose I take a job offer, one over another. I'm extremely successful in the company and get an immediate raise. I marry this person instead of that person and it is one of those blissful, happily-ever-after marriages. I buy a house that appreciates in value at 40 percent per year even when nobody else's does. Does that mean in every case I've made the right choice according to God's will?

What if I take a job that is difficult day in and day out? The company is in trouble, and my salary goes down. What if I marry a person I deeply love, and it is an exceptionally difficult marriage? The house value plummets. Do these outcomes mean I chose outside of God's will?

Remember that virtually all of the people who wrote the books of the New Testament died as martyrs. That is hardly a comfortable outcome. Their lives, even before their deaths, were not always simple or easy.

Christians live by faith. We trust God for the outcome. So we take each of these steps. We love God, follow the Bible, pray for wisdom, get good counsel, decide as best we can, and then leave the rest to God. If our choice leads to an outcome that is less pleasant than we would have projected, we still seek to live faithfully. No matter what happens, we trust God. That's the Christian way of making decisions.

Take the long distance view

Recently, Charleen and I were talking about our years of marriage together. (We were married younger than I would advise people to get married today, so there was a lot to talk about.) It was a "Did you ever think that—?" conversation.

"Did you ever think that we would live in the places that we lived?"

"Charleen, did you ever think that you would work for a daily newspaper?"

"Leith, did you ever think that you'd become a mobile home repairman?"

"Did you ever think we'd be at a university in Illinois and graduate school in Colorado?"

"Did you ever think that we'd end up in Minnesota?"

On our wedding day, these were not events plotted on our list of future hopes and dreams. (As a native of New Jersey, I'm not sure I even knew where Minnesota was located.) We had no idea how life would progress—what paths we would take, what decisions we would make, and how it would all come together. But we stood during our wedding and said that we would love each other for richer, for poorer, for better, for worse, in sickness and in health, until death us do part.

Our marriage is about relationship, not primarily about the specific decisions that we have made together. Decisions are important, of course, but always in the context of relationship. Charleen and I even forget what the decisions were! A decade ago we were involved in what seemed like an agonizing decision—how to landscape our yard. Yet, when I think about the experience now, I can barely remember it. "Do you remember how much that cost?" I asked Charleen. She had no idea. What seemed like a significant decision then is now lost in time. The relationship—that's what continues.

Keep relationship at the core

A Christian is someone who has a personal relationship with God through Jesus Christ. That relationship should make all the difference in how that person behaves and thinks. Being a Christian is not most about career or marriage or house or any of those things. It's most about a relationship with God.

So when making the important decisions of life, we need to worry less about the outcome and concern ourselves more with building and growing this most important relationship. To be a Christian is to be wholeheartedly committed to God and to live life for God. In this relationship, we will have riches and poverty. We will have sickness and health. We will have good times and bad times. We will get some decisions right and others wrong. Through it all, we can lean on our relationship with God. Life isn't about us. It's about God. When faced with difficult decisions—today or in the future—our relationship with God is our most valuable advantage.

Part Three: Christian Strength... Persevering through Difficulty

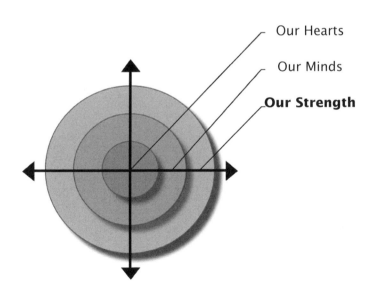

Our Hearts

Our Minds

Our Strength

Chapter Seven

Coping with Criticism

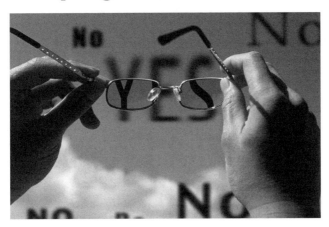

Ethel, a devoted wife, sat beside her husband's hospital bed, holding his weak and wrinkled hand. She had been married to Stan for fifty-five years, and he was seriously ill. She wasn't going anywhere.

"Is that you, Ethel, at my side again?" Stan whispered.

"Yes, dear," she answered softly. "I'm here."

Stan spoke haltingly to his wife of a lifetime, "Remember, years ago, when I was injured and laid up in the Veteran's Hospital? You were with me then. Remember when we lost everything in that terrible fire? You were with me then. And Ethel, when we were poor, you never left my side." Stan sighed deeply. "I tell you, Ethel, you have been nothing but bad luck."[22]

Facing the inevitable

Have you ever felt like Ethel—giving and giving, then getting blindsided by criticism?

Criticism is faultfinding, and I am confident that every person experiences it sooner or later. Criticism can be nit-picky and merely annoying, or it can be demeaning, demoralizing, and even devastating. We often think of criticism taking place behind our backs, which is bad enough, but that's not always the case. Criticism can also be delivered right to our faces.

Criticism hurts. Whether given with the utmost sensitivity or excruciating harshness, it can be extremely difficult to take—especially when we know the critique is valid or carries even a hint of truth. We cringe, withdraw, and try our best to avoid hearing it.

Years ago, I was on the board of directors of an organization that hired Christians for a variety of ministries across North America. People who were listed in the reference section of the application were asked to rate how the applicant handled criticism. Their responses were not very encouraging! Across the board, this was one of the lowest ratings. I don't remember any candidate who was described as enjoying criticism or appreciative and enthusiastic about receiving it.

But criticism is a part of life that we've all experienced—on the job, with our family and friends, and in our churches. (If we're honest, we must admit that we have all criticized others as well.) How, as Christians, are we supposed to deal with criticism of our actions, our words, and sometimes our very selves? When we love God and want to act like Christians in every part of life, how do we cope?

Feeling reproached? Join the crowd

As human targets for painful criticism, we're in good company. Nehemiah was one of the greatest leaders of ancient history, the trusted confidant of King Artaxerxes of Persia. He was also the agent of God who took on the enormous job of rebuilding the city of Jerusalem, which had been left in terrible disrepair. He was a good man on a great mission, and yet he faced severe criticism.

St. Paul wrote more books of the New Testament than any other author. He was a successful missionary, church planter, theologian, and apostle. Yet he was so severely criticized by people in the churches he started that he spent much precious writing time defending himself in answer to his critics.

Moses was a courageous emissary to the Egyptian pharaoh, a man who risked his neck to demand freedom for the enslaved Israelites. Once he secured their liberty with God's help, he led them on a perilous journey to the land that had been promised to them by God. But did he receive compliments or gratitude for this work? No, he got reproach, judgment, criticism, and griping.

Jesus, who never sinned, was called a drunk, a liar, and a tool of the devil.

Even the best of people—those trying to live godly lives—have been forced to cope with criticism. What can we learn from them? What does the Bible tell us? How will people recognize that we are *different* by our reactions to the criticism that is sure to come during our lifetimes?

Guidelines for a godly response

Dealing gracefully with criticism may never be easy, but being prepared is greatly helpful. Expect to be criticized during your lifetime, and get ready now. Here are a few pointers.

Listen to the criticism. I need to qualify this suggestion by adding the phrase: "most of the time." There is some faultfinding that is neither instructive nor positive. For example, after many years of experience, I have chosen not to receive or read anonymous criticisms—or anonymous messages. If there is no name or return address on an envelope, I open it and look for a signature at the end. If there is no signature, I throw the letter away unread. If I receive e-mail from an unknown source, I delete it without opening it. If someone leaves an article or book for me to read, and I don't know where it came from, I throw it away. It's hard to have a positive dialogue with someone who chooses to criticize anonymously.

But when the letter is signed, an individual addresses me face-to-face, or I get a personal phone call, what then? What would *you* do? As Christians, we respect other people and hear what they have to say. The Bible gives us our guideline: *"My dear brothers and sisters, take note of this: Everyone should be quick to listen, slow to speak and slow to become angry"* (James 1:19). Why listen to criticism? We should hear out our critics and humbly consider what they have to say because, sometimes, they are right!

Take, for example, the Old Testament prophet, Nathan, who dared to confront King David about his blatant adultery and murder. Nathan's actions took courage, for it is neither easy nor safe to confront a powerful king. He could have lost his life. But David needed to hear the truth, and, to his credit, he listened. The prophet's indictment of David's behavior was both creative and specific (read 2 Samuel 12:1-11), and King David's response was stunning. *"Then David said to Nathan, 'I have sinned against the LORD'"* (2 Samuel 12:13).

If you, like David, are in a position to receive criticism, first hear what your critic says. Restate the criticism back to that person to be sure you correctly understand. Remember that listening doesn't mean acknowledging that this individual is correct in the assessment. It doesn't even mean that you believe he's criticizing you in the right way. It does demonstrate your willingness to humbly listen—an act that is Christ-like.

Give a slow gentle response. That's the whole point in James 1:19: *"slow to speak and slow to become angry."* Look at Proverbs 15:1 for another benefit: *"A gentle answer turns away wrath, but a harsh word stirs up anger."* More wisdom appears in Proverbs 12:16: *"Fools show their annoyance at once, but the prudent overlook an insult."* So even when you feel insulted or criticized, take it slow, take a deep breath, pray a quick prayer, and think through your response. Don't escalate a potentially explosive situation; diffuse it. With God's help, you can turn a difficult experience into something positive by the way you respond.

Consider the source. It is tempting to think only of ourselves—our dignity, self-esteem, and feelings—when we are criticized, but as Christians we also need to think about our critics. Ask yourself, "What is happening in this person's life?" "Why is she so angry?" "What is his need?" Philippians 2:4-5 reminds us, *"In humility, value others above yourselves, not looking to your own interests but each of you to the interests of others. In your relationships with one another, have the same attitude of mind Christ Jesus had."* While this is not always an easy practice, it is one that brings us closer to Christ in attitude and behavior.

Early in my tenure as pastor of a church, a man made an appointment to come to my office. I had no clue as to what was the purpose of the meeting. Within the first minute or two of our conversation, however, I started to get a pretty clear idea. He handed me a pile of photocopied sheets about "How to Accept Criticism." I took the pages from him and set them on the table next to me to read later. He said, "No, you need to read these right now." I picked up the sheets and read them, and in my heart I had a sinking feeling about where this conversation was headed.

Once I had read the papers, this man opened a spiral-bound subject notebook devoted entirely to criticisms of me. He was a very organized individual, so he had the items set up by subject matter. It took him over an hour to thoroughly cover his detailed critiques of my preaching, grammar, programs, and what he didn't like about me personally. I listened carefully and took notes, trying hard not be defensive, trying to listen and learn. When he was finished I asked, "What do you think is my greatest problem—that I am incompetent or ungodly?" He thought about it for a while and then said, "It's both—you are ungodly *and* incompetent."

For weeks and maybe months, I reflected on what he had said because I was afraid he was right. I thought that he could see the faults in me that I could not see in myself. I wondered if he was the kind of person who could pierce through the veneer and see hidden sins. What I failed to do, at least at first, is to consider this individual's needs and motivation.

Often criticism has little to do with you and everything to do with the critic. Some people don't know how hurtful their words are. They've never learned to be kind. They're not just that way with you; they're that way with others. We sometimes need to feel sorry for the critic rather than angry or defensive.

Strong anger may be a sign that something else is going on in the critic's life—lost employment, poor health, low self-esteem, frustration, or failure. All these may burst out in criticism against others. You may be a safe and convenient target. People who are hurt often act out against parents, teachers, friends, or persons in positions of authority. You may be criticized because of who you are, not because of what you have done.

So, what is our response? Look at these seemingly contradictory proverbs that stand back-to-back in Proverbs 26:4-5: *"Do not answer fools according to their folly, or you will be just like them. Answer fools according to their folly or they will be wise in their own eyes."* What's the point here? Different people require different answers, and different situations call for different responses. Sometimes we should say nothing, particularly to people who are habitually critical. You know them. They have a harsh word about everyone and everything. They have criticized you and others repeatedly. We should not reward their dysfunction by taking their words as seriously as the thoughtful, loving, careful, and occasional critic. On the other hand, we should sometimes defend ourselves or correct the person whose words are foolish. So make an assessment before deciding how to respond to a critic. Analyze the critic and the criticism.

Get counsel. Before rushing into a confrontation with someone who has been critical of you, look for wise advice:

- Start by asking God for wisdom. Pray. Tell God what has happened. Pour out your feelings and thoughts. Ask God to give you wise ideas on how to act like a Christian in the present circumstance. Ask God if you should answer your critic or just let it go.

- Talk with a trusted, godly person who you know can keep a confidence. (The last thing you need is to fan the fire by having others gossiping about this issue.) Share your concerns with this mature fellow Christian, especially if you have been deeply hurt by the criticism you have received. Perhaps you're feeling defensive and angry. Talking to a strong and insightful fellow believer can help to settle you down and assist you in regaining the perspective of a Christian, someone who responds as Christ would respond. Process what has been said, evaluate possible responses, and allow your friend to pray with you before you move ahead. Your Christian friend can read your e-mail before it is sent, edit your letter before it is mailed, and listen to you practice your response before you speak. Time after time I have been helped by fellow Christians who have listened and then encouraged me to respond with strength and love. They have counseled me either to accept the criticism (and make a necessary change in my life or behavior) or to laugh it off as foolishness. Seeking counsel is a recurring biblical theme and simply a wise action to take.

Bless your critics. When criticism is especially mean-spirited and cruel, we have a special charge from Jesus: "*Love your enemies, do good to those who hate you, bless those who curse you, pray for those who mistreat you*" (Luke 6:27-28). In other words, when your critics are at their most vicious state, bless them with kindness. It doesn't matter whether their criticisms are right or wrong.

This could be one of the hardest, but also one of the most Christian, things we'll ever do. It's a choice—curse or bless—and the Bible clearly indicates which way a Christian should choose. "*Bless those who persecute you; bless and do not curse*" (Romans 12:14). Don't think you can do it? Even when you feel attacked and vulnerable, God can give you the power to respond with goodness, and the rewards will be incredible. Proverbs 12:18 tells us, "*The words of the reckless pierce like swords, but the tongue of the wise brings healing.*"

Jesus said that one way to bless our cruelest critics is to pray for them. No, he didn't mean that we should pray for them to choke on a chicken bone or be run over by a truck. He asked us to pray for their well-being. By praying, we are trusting God to turn a terrible situation into good, rather than following our own instincts to get even. You may be amazed at the difference God makes when you pray in response to criticism instead of allowing yourself to become angry, depressed, or upset.

Author and businessman Fred Smith tells about a friend who was "emotionally crucified by his critics." Smith says that these critics had profited from his friend and owed him gratitude, not criticism. When his friend died, Fred Smith paged through the man's Bible and found a prayer list. At the top of the list was written, "Pray for those who are lying about me."[23] How completely Christian!

Try to avoid stirring up criticism. As a pastor, I've experienced my share of criticism in ministry. Along the way I've learned to head off some criticisms before they can materialize. I know there are some ways of saying and doing things that set some people off. There are stories that trigger anger among people who are looking for things to criticize. So I look for ways to accomplish God's purposes and teach God's truth and keep those critics at bay. It's an idea from the Bible. In 2 Corinthians 8:20-21, Paul made an extra effort to head off the criticism before it came, realizing that money matters trigger criticism. He was far-sighted in his approach.

We want to avoid any criticism of the way we administer this liberal gift. For we are taking pains to do what is right, not only in the eyes of the Lord but also in the eyes of others.

Being sensitive and far-sighted does not mean avoiding difficult topics, telling untruths or sidestepping biblical truth, but it may mean not tweaking someone's nose just to get a rise.

Avoid making matters worse. There is a temptation to respond to criticism in ways that will make matters far worse in the future. Some people become their own worst enemies in this regard. So don't lose your temper in writing—or in any way!

Think about those who respond to a critical e-mail with angry words. The e-mail is forwarded and copied until dozens more people are involved. I have tried to follow a policy of never writing anything I wouldn't want read in public a year or a decade later.

Take the long view. When dealing with the inevitable criticisms of life, don't be shortsighted. With God's help, take the long view. The best long-term response to a critic is a life well lived and a job well done.

Colonel George Washington Goethals directed the building of the Panama Canal. He faced formidable problems even beyond the enormous technical challenges of constructing the huge locks, the bad weather, the natural barriers of geography, and the logistical nightmare of housing and caring for over 30,000 workers. His biggest burden was the severe criticism from people, politicians, and the press back at home. A co-worker asked him when he was going to answer his critics, and Goethals replied, "In time." His friend persisted: *"When?"* The colonel said, "When the canal is finished."[24]

While that exact tactic may not always be possible for us, the principle is sound. We need to be patient and wait for the outcome. Here's how Peter puts it: *"Live such good lives among the pagans that, though they accuse you of doing wrong, they may see your good deeds and glorify God on the day he visits us"* (1 Peter 2:12). Now substitute the word critics for pagans. *"Live such good lives among [your critics] that, though they accuse you of doing wrong, they may see your good deeds and glorify God on the day he visits us."*

Teach others. One of the very best long-term Christian actions is to teach others how to effectively and lovingly criticize. Many people don't know how to confront in a healthy way. They grew up in families where they were constantly torn down, and that's all they know how to do. So model Christian criticism for others to learn. Speak the truth in love. Be kind. Never criticize anonymously. Avoid anger. Be constructive and helpful.

Check your own criticisms by the response you get. Do others thank you for your insights? Do they smile? Do they know that you love them and care for them? Do they agree that you did the right thing? Of course, it's not always possible to get a positive reaction in response to criticism, but it is what Christian criticism should always seek. Be the kind of critic that others wish to emulate, the kind that others trust and thank God for.

Most often—let this be your guide—keep quiet.

And if you can't criticize well, don't criticize at all.

If you've been hurt...

Finally, a special word to those who have been deeply hurt by the criticisms of others: We must acknowledge that criticism can create wounds that will never heal. Criticism can leave people discouraged, crushed, and hopeless.

If you've suffered that sort of criticism, realize that God knows you better than anyone else. God knows your strengths and weaknesses, your successes and failures. And—no matter what—God loves you. God reaches out to help and heal, to encourage and bless, to lift you over the worst of critics and criticisms and bless you with unconditional love.

If your unkind critics were your parents, let God be your affirming Father.

If you have been crushed by the words of an employer, let God be your encouraging boss.

If you have been devastated by the words of a husband or wife, let God be the lover of your soul.

If someone you trusted has attacked you, let God be your best friend.

And when you face criticism, may the Holy Spirit fill you and help you to act like Jesus Christ.

Chapter Eight

Facing Serious Illness

No one wants to suffer.

No one wants to die.

Even Jesus didn't. The night before his death he pleaded with God. He referred to his own suffering and death as his cup and prayed, *"My Father, if it is possible, may this cup be taken from me"* (Matthew 26:39).

Even though we don't want suffering, sickness, or death, we all face these moments. The circumstances and the intensity of the suffering vary, but we all eventually experience pain, illness, uncertainty, and death. Books are written, sermons preached, and classes conducted to explain why bad things happen to good people, why innocent people suffer in a world where God is ultimately sovereign.

How do we respond as Christians when terrible things happen? What is a Christian to do when diagnosed with cancer, struggling with depression, in chronic pain, or dealing with a malady no one would ever choose? How are we to be *Christian* during serious illness?

There are no easy answers to these questions, but we can build a list of behaviors that Christians might exhibit when suffering.

Behavior #1: Christians turn to God

God is there the minute we hurt, the day the diagnosis comes, and the instant our world changes forever. We might be so scared that we can hardly speak. We might be filled with uncertainty, dread, and denial. But we go to God and pour out our hearts. That's what Christians do.

Hezekiah was the thirty-nine-year-old king of Israel who became desperately ill. The prophet Isaiah came to his home and said the words no patient ever wants to hear.

> *"In those days Hezekiah became ill and was at the point of death. The prophet Isaiah son of Amoz went to him and said, 'This is what the LORD says: Put your house in order, because you are going to die; you will not recover"* (2 Kings 20:1).

Hezekiah was given a terrible prognosis, and he was scared. His heart was broken. His mind was reeling. Weeping bitterly, he tried to bargain with God. He reminded God that he had been a good man. He pleaded for his life: "*Remember, LORD, how I have walked before you faithfully and with wholehearted devotion and have done what is good in your eyes*" (2 Kings 20:3). Hezekiah did what godly people always do when told that they are going to die. He turned his face to the wall and poured his heart out to God.

If I had been in Hezekiah's place, I would have done exactly the same thing. I would have chased everybody out of the room so I could cry out to God. "Not now! Not like this! God, there has got to be some other way." I would be far more filled with emotion than rational thinking. I'd pour my heart out to him and ask for help, over and over. "God, no, please, please, please! Not now! Not me!" I would implore God, because that is what

Christians do when we face the uncontrollable things of life. We trust God and tell God what's on our hearts. It is how Christians act in the face of serious illness.

What did God do for Hezekiah? *"Before Isaiah had left the middle court, the word of the LORD came to him: 'Go back and tell Hezekiah the leader of my people, "This is what the LORD, the God of your father David says: I have heard your prayer and seen your tears; I will heal you. On the third day from now you will go up to the temple of the LORD. I will add fifteen years to your life"'"*(2 Kings 20:4-6a).

So God gave some amazingly good news to Hezekiah—a fifteen-year extension. It's not always like that. In fact, it's not often like that. But God can turn a final prognosis of death into life. God can and sometimes does intervene and heal people.

Does God owe me? Should I say (like Hezekiah), "God you know I've been a good person. I've done a lot of good things. If there is anybody you should give life to, it ought to be me"? I don't think I would have any right to say that. (I might say it, but I don't have any right to say it.) God does heal some people. But I also know that Christians get sick and die just as everyone else gets sick and dies.

In fact, Hezekiah remained desperately ill for three more days. Even after he had received this promise from God, there was no indication that God was going to come through. But at thirty-nine years of age, Hezekiah had a guarantee of life to somewhere around his fifty-fourth birthday. It must have sounded like a wonderfully long time—for a while. So how old are you? Add fifteen years to your age and decide if you think that would be enough life for you. That's the reality that Hezekiah faced.

Behavior #2: Christians accept medical help

For Hezekiah, it wasn't a direct healing. In fact, God specifically instructed him to get the best medical treatment available. Isaiah told him to prepare a poultice of figs. The poultice was prepared and applied to the boil—to whatever infection he had—and he recovered.

From my perspective in the twenty-first century, I think, "What possible good was that going to do?" It was a paste made of figs and applied to his skin! By any modern standard of science, this was folk medicine at its most primitive. But that's not the point. The point is that God told Hezekiah to go to the doctor, and he did. God had already decided to supernaturally intervene, but God still used the best of human resources that were available to people at that time.

So, as Christians, how do we act when facing serious illness? We turn to God; then we take our medicine. It's not either/or. It's prayer and the poultice. It's prayer and penicillin. It's God first and the doctor too. We pour our hearts out to God, and we get the medical help that God provides.

Behavior #3: Christians live for Jesus

When we face serious illness and suffering, we, unlike Hezekiah, don't know how long we have. We don't know if we have a day, a month, a decade, or longer. I've often thought it's a very good thing that I don't know the day that I'm going to die. I think it would cast a shadow over the rest of life that would be far more negative than positive. But what we do know is that every day we live, every extension we have—whether fifteen minutes, two hours, five days, ten months, or fifty years—is a gift from God, and we are to live every one of those minutes, hours, days, months, and years for him.

Of course, we prefer that all of our days, however long we are going to live, are really good days. We want them to be pleasurable and problem free. Most of our days *are* good days. Certainly when life is good, we should live for the glory of God—we should live to enhance God's reputation. But when the days are painful, frightening, or difficult, we should also live for God. Christians should consider every day to be a gift from God.

In Philippians 1:27, Paul writes, *"Whatever happens, as citizens of heaven live in a manner worthy of the gospel of Christ."* In other words, we are to make God look good no matter what happens. And some of what happens is likely to be hard. Two verses later, Paul adds, *"It has been granted to you on behalf of Christ not only to believe on him, but also to suffer for him"* (Philippians 1:29). And there we have the core of Christianity. We are to live for Jesus and conduct our lives in a way that is aligned with him and honors him. We are to live out our Christian faith in the very best of days when we want to sing, shout and celebrate, and in the very worst of days filled with danger, despair and grief.

Writing those words scares me. I'm afraid that they will echo in my mind the day after I'm in a terrible car accident and discover that I'm paralyzed for the rest of my life. I'm afraid that someone will open this book and show me this page the week that I'm diagnosed with cancer. I'm afraid that when I am in the pits of clinical depression, I'll page through my Bible and find the verses that I've shared with you and realize that I can't do what I've told you to do. What if, in the midst of paralysis or cancer or depression or some other hated and unanticipated trauma of life, I can't live for Jesus Christ?

But that question brings us right back again to the core of Christianity. We live not by our own strength but by the strength of Jesus Christ. We live by faith. We are convinced that God is a God of grace. God will be there. When we need strength, God will give us the strength, courage, help, and hope that we need for that suffering. God will not abandon us. God has no intention or expectation that we go through difficulty alone. God may not give to any of us the same answer that God gave to Hezekiah—that quick turnaround from predicted death to a fifteen-year extension—but God will be there. Just as God was there for Hezekiah, God will be there for us.

Behavior #4: Christians grow through difficulty

This next point doesn't make sense to unbelievers. When we suffer, we have the opportunity to grow as Christians, a chance we would not otherwise have. Suffering can bring us closer to Jesus. Only a Christian could understand this. When we suffer, we somehow connect to him and have a deeper appreciation of how he suffered horribly for us. We make a spiritual, even a supernatural connection. We taste a little bit of his suffering. Peter writes:

> *Praise be to the God and Father of our Lord Jesus Christ! In his great mercy he has given us new birth into a living hope through the resurrection of Jesus Christ from the dead... In this you greatly rejoice, though now for a little while you may have had to suffer grief in all kinds of trials. These have come so that your faith—of greater worth than gold, which perishes even though refined by fire—may be proved genuine and may result in praise, glory and honor when Jesus Christ is revealed. Though you have not seen him, you love him; and even though you do not see him now, you believe in him and are filled with an inexpressible and glorious joy, for you are receiving the end result of your faith, the salvation of your souls.* (1 Peter 1:3, 6-9)

When Christians suffer, we know that as terrible as it is, *the suffering is temporary*. There will be a release followed by eternity.

When Christians suffer, *we have our faith tested and confirmed*. This gives us a confidence that would not be possible in the midst of a life of ease.

When Christians suffer, *we grow closer to Jesus* than we ever would have if life had been problem free. We would never choose suffering, but that's how we handle it. That's how we act as Christians. For some, the growth is in trusting God to provide daily needs in the midst of that pain and suffering. It is something like the manna that God sent to the people of Israel when they were lost in the wilderness. (See Exodus 16.)

Jeffrey Boyd is a medical doctor practicing in Waterbury, Connecticut. He tells the story of his wife who did not receive the healing that Hezekiah received.

My first wife, Pat, had diabetes, two heart attacks, bypass surgery, two strokes, went on dialysis, went blind, and had both legs amputated above the knee. She and I went every week to a healing service at our church. The clergy would lay hands on us and pray while Pat and I cried uncontrollably. She was never healed. There was no evidence that healing prayer had any positive effect in terms of miraculous cures. But every week this intimate prayer gave us enough spiritual strength to endure another week. Thus my own experience was that healing prayer was like manna for Pat and me. Every Sunday we were given enough to get us through. We were not given more nor less manna than we needed to survive. It was exactly like Exodus 16 and like the Lord's Prayer, "Give us today our daily bread."

In other words Pat and I experienced healing prayer to have a curative power not in terms in a change of medical outcome, but in terms of keeping us in touch with our Lord, who spiritually sustained us.[25]

If none of this sounds easy, it's because it *isn't* easy. Serious illness and suffering never are. Yet in suffering we have the opportunity to act as Christians—to tell God what's on our hearts, to get the medical help that God provides, to live life that God has granted, and to grow.

Helping the hurting

I have one more list. It's not for those who are sick. It's for those who are healthy. This is advice on how a Christian acts toward people who are seriously ill and suffering.

See the person and not the sickness. Please don't define someone by his or her disease or disability. Whether someone is suffering from a mental illness or a physical injury, always treat the sufferer with respect as a person, not as a malady.

Realize that looking okay on the outside doesn't mean being okay on the inside. I often say to people, and I mean well when I say it, "You look great today." But I need to be cautious. I need to be sensitive to the soul as well as the appearance of the face because sometimes the way we look on the outside is not the way we feel on the inside.

We need to remember that chronic pain varies. Just because someone is having a good afternoon doesn't mean that the morning was good. Just because the afternoon is pain-free doesn't mean that there will not be a painful and sleepless night.

Understand that depression is a frequent side effect of suffering. Our bodies, minds, and souls are all wired together. That's God's design. Understand that the best of people become clinically depressed.

Beware of playing doctor. Resist the temptation to second-guess what the physicians have said or to recommend some alternate theory or alternative medicine.

Don't play God. Sometimes those who are on the outside of suffering and serious illness want to offer explanations: "Maybe you sinned." That was the explanation that was given to Job. People who aren't suffering must resist the temptation to say, "If you would confess your sin, then you would get to be a whole lot better." When we play God, we're assuming we have a supernatural perspective we really don't have.

Offer emotional support. Just be there. Recognize that as the friend or the family of those who are suffering, we don't have to cure them. That's not our job. We need to be there, to be a comfort and a friend.

Say that you will pray, and to do it. People who are seriously ill may not be very good at praying for themselves. You can be the one who will pray on their behalf. Pray your suffering friend or family member through the pain. Pray through the discouragement. Pray for the caregivers. Pray with zeal and persistence. Don't just say it, but do it. Pray.

Facing the future, but not alone

On November 5, 1994 former President Ronald Reagan wrote a letter to the American people:

> I have recently been told that I am one of the millions of Americans who will be afflicted with Alzheimer's disease.
>
> So, now we feel it is important to share it with you.
>
> At the moment I feel just fine. I intend to live the remainder of the years God gives me on earth doing the things I've always done.
>
> Unfortunately, as Alzheimer's disease progresses the family often bears a heavy burden.
>
> I now begin the journey that will lead me into the sunset of my life.
>
> > May God always bless you.
> > Sincerely, Ronald Reagan [26]

When facing serious illness, when suffering great pain, when beginning our own journey into the sunset of life, may we trust God and may we, with the help of God's Holy Spirit, act distinctively like Christians in the midst of the difficulty.

Chapter Nine

Grieving Great Losses

For David, it was a day of unspeakable grief. The nation was torn by civil war. Twenty thousand men had died in one of the bloodiest battles of history. And although he had been anointed by God to be the king of Israel, David had lost the support of most of the nation, not to mention most of his own army. He was a fugitive on the run from insurrection led by his son! Absalom had already murdered his brother and was now threatening to kill his father in order to gain the throne.

David fled Jerusalem, Israel's capital city, with a small army of loyal and experienced soldiers. The battle was looming, and the prospects of success for David's army were slim. In fact, his generals advised him to stay behind because it was likely that he would be captured or killed.

Reluctantly, David watched as his army marched off to the battle. But before the fight began, he pulled his generals aside and whispered a last wish and order to each of them: *"Be gentle with the young man Absalom for my sake"* (2 Samuel 18:5). There was nothing left to do now but wait.

David anxiously awaited news. There were two runners, two of the fastest in his army. As the battle progressed, they each came with different kinds of news. The first runner arrived. "Good news! Very good news! Although the battle was bloody, you are victorious. The kingdom is preserved. The crown is still yours. God has triumphed greatly in Israel this day." But the second runner approached David and said, "Your son, Absalom, is dead."

The king went up to the room over the gateway and wailed with grief. *"O my son, Absalom! My son, my son, Absalom! If only I had died instead of you—O Absalom, my son, my son!"* (2 Samuel 18:33) David would never see Absalom again. He would never walk with him. He would never talk with him. Absalom would never succeed him on the throne. Absalom would never have a son of his own.

But this son was a traitor! A murderer! He wanted to kill his father! Any rational person would say that Absalom got exactly what he deserved. But that day, David wasn't thinking about politics or justice or the kingdom. He was thinking about his son, whom he had lost forever.

Reeling from the loss

Grief is like that—seldom rational, always emotional. Grief is our response to the greatest losses of life, and it comes in all different sizes, shapes, and packages.

Grief is what happens when you lose a job that you loved. You did your very best, and now you have no idea how you're going to make it without a paycheck or benefits.

Grief comes after the divorce. You loved each other. Once it was a dream come true—"happily every after." What began with so much promise ended with hatred and acrimony.

Grief can result from lost finances. Life savings are spent, the stock has disappeared, or the company has gone bankrupt. The money is gone, and so is everything that went with it—the promises, plans, and expectations. Life from now on is going to be different.

Grief comes with disability. There is a loss that medicine cannot repair and surgery cannot fix. Everybody else seems to have it better. They can see; you can't. They can walk; you'll never walk again. They have the dexterity you have lost or the speech you wish you could have. Every day brings memories of the person you once were and never will be again.

Grief comes with the end of a relationship that was important. You trusted someone and were betrayed. You loved and were hurt.

And there's the grief that comes with death, the cruelest and most final of losses. Everything that you had hoped for is taken away. There is a finality that defies words.

We all have hopes and dreams that are stolen or shattered. Sometimes it is a long process. Sometimes it is sudden and unexpected. The circumstances of life deliver a body blow that sends you reeling. You lose your equilibrium and wonder if you can ever go on with life.

The symptoms of grief

Grief is our response to those losses. It's a mix of emotions—feelings of overwhelming sadness, hurt, anger, and depression all at the same time. One moment you want to get even by fighting back, and the next moment you want to curl up in a fetal position and die.

Grief often brings actual, physical pain. There can be shortness of breath, heart palpitations, change in heart rate, headaches, and insomnia. The symptoms can be unpredictable. A psychologist once told me that on the day you think everything is fine—that you're over it and finally okay—grief sneaks up behind you with a two-by-four and slams you over the head. You never knew what was coming. You're driving down the highway, you see another car, and it reminds you. You hear a tune on the radio, and it brings those cascading memories all over again. In our autobiographies, we all have these stories of grief.

Looking for help

Our culture has many ways of trying to help—but not all are helpful.

I find that it is often not helpful to hear the stories of others. Psychologists refer to this as "comparing pain." Somebody else comes along with a story of a situation different or far worse. It seems to diminish the pain that we feel, as if it doesn't count. Or we're told about another person who faced what we're facing. *She* handled the situation victoriously, triumphantly, and with apparent ease.

Well-meaning people say that time heals all wounds. Time *can* help. But there are some wounds that never close up. They never heal. When someone we love dies, there are no replacements.

You go through a divorce, and in the midst of the agony that comes with the loss, a friend trying to be helpful says, "Aw, don't worry. There are plenty of fish in the sea. Somebody else will come along." You want to scream back, "You don't get it! You don't understand! You don't know what this feels like!"

Some people tell us to tough it out. "That's how things go. Don't be a crybaby. Get on with your life." While there may be a kernel of truth in that advice, it's hard to hear those words from someone who isn't suffering what *we're* suffering.

Grief in small-town Colorado

I first learned about grief as a twenty-four-year-old seminary graduate when I became a pastor of a church in a small Colorado city. There were two hundred people in the church. This particular community had more nursing home beds per capita than any other place in the state. People I didn't even know often called upon me to officiate at funerals, pray, offer words of wisdom, and sit beside the bed of individuals who were dying. I saw someone die for the first time. This wasn't television. It was real. Suddenly I had firsthand and first-time experiences with grief, and I was not prepared for these real life responsibilities.

I had to deliver terrible news. I remember parking in a driveway, walking up to the door, and ringing the bell. The people who opened the door and greeted me were warm, friendly, and laughing. I heard myself say, "Could we sit down a moment? I have some difficult news to tell you."

There were suicides that left families devastated.

There were accidents. A young man who grew up in the church offered to fly a group of others from one Colorado city to another. He didn't have an instrument rating and was caught in a snow squall. He flew that plane at more than two hundred miles an hour straight into the ground. He left a young widow and child.

I was in over my head, way over my head.

I did the best I could, often with a quivering voice, shaking hands, and a sense of inadequacy. And I learned a lot of lessons. I learned that not everyone grieves alike. Some people scream. Some people don't say a word. Some people seem to process quickly. Some people seem to never get over their grief.

Is there such a thing as Christian grief?

But one thing stood out. There *is* a difference between the grief of Christians and the grief of those who aren't Christians. It's a tangible and obvious difference. I saw it in emergency rooms and hospitals, in county courtrooms, and at gravesides. Christians grieved differently because they had hope. Even in fairly new Christians, even in some who I considered to be immature in their faith and not particularly devout, I sensed the difference—the presence of the Holy Spirit, the movement of God, the nature of their grief. It was amazing to witness.

Paul pinpoints this difference in 1 Thessalonians 4:13 when he writes, *"Brothers and sisters, we do not want you to...grieve like the rest, who have no hope."* His point is simple and significant.

We do not deny that there's been a loss. We don't say there is an absence of grief. But there is a deep-down connection with God that gives hope. There is an expectation of a better tomorrow, the trust that God will make a difference. God may not change the immediate circumstance, but he will be there. Tomorrow will be different. Tomorrow will be better.

Christians grieve, but in the midst of our grief we believe that God exists, that God knows what's happening, and that God understands. Recognizing God's presence makes all the difference in the world. Even Christians who are angry with God—who lash out and say, "God, where were you? What were you thinking? Why did you allow this to happen to me?"—are acknowledging belief in God. And while that anger may last for a time, belief transcends even the moment of anger. We believe that God provides sufficient grace. Grace is the special provision given to Christians—for whatever circumstances we face.

Paul, a fellow sufferer

The apostle Paul, who struggled with a physical disability, knew about grief. When he encountered other people, he envied them. He wanted to be whole in the same way that they were whole. He didn't want his disability, and he repeatedly pleaded that God would take it away. Over and over God simply said "No." Finally, in resignation and wisdom, Paul recorded the words of Jesus. *"My grace is sufficient for you, for my power is made perfect in weakness"* (2 Corinthians 12:9a). Paul discovered that when he was at his weakest, the adequacy of the grace of God was at its peak.

Maybe you do what I sometimes do. I imagine terrible things happening to me. I wonder, "What would be my response if it were *my* diagnosis, *my* impending death, *my* child, *my* marriage, *my* job, or *my* life?" "I couldn't deal with it," I tell myself. "I couldn't do half as well as the people I see going through crises that I imagine might someday happen to me."

And then I realize that God gives grace when the time comes, not in advance. I can't store it up. God will offer grace that is sufficient when that time actually comes.

Grace: God's "right time" gift

As Christians, we grieve knowing that God will provide sufficient grace, even if we can't imagine it at the moment. It will be adequate, for God will give it when we need it. It is a promise and an expectation.

That doesn't stop us from praying for a change in our circumstances. We say, "God, switch it around. Fix the relationship; provide the money; heal the disease; make this go away." And God often does. You know the stories. You've had it happen in your own life. Between us we could come up with hundreds of examples of terrible situations that God turned around.

But sometimes God doesn't change the outcome. Sometimes the grief is final. It doesn't turn into happiness. The dreams are shattered, and there are no other dreams that will replace them. But still we have an ultimate hope. As Christians, our perspective is clear. It's hard and painful now. It may be difficult for a decade or decades to come. But in the broad perspective of eternity, we claim the promise in Revelation 7:17: *"God will wipe away every tear from their eyes."* Someday there will be no more death, mourning, crying, or pain. The old order of things will pass away. That's what lies deep down inside the grief of the Christian: hope. Hope is an expectation that ultimately God will make everything good.

Grieving together

Until then—for now—we are never alone. We grieve with a family of faith. We have other Christians and the church. Of course, by "church," I don't mean a building or an institution. I mean relationships. Again, we could gather thousands upon thousands of testimonials of those who have gone through the deepest waters. But they didn't go alone. Fellow Christians have been there, prayed, provided, met needs, and been the channels and the agents of the grace of God through those worst of times. That's God's gift to us: We are part of a family that is headed by Jesus Christ.

Get prepared

The time to make that connection is before the tragedy strikes. In my work I will sometimes receive a telephone call from someone who identifies with the congregation but has stayed on the periphery. He's been caught up in the busyness of life and has never had the time to meet people, fill out an information card, join the church, become part of a class or a support group, or involve his children or family. Life has been good and full. Life has been fine. And then tragedy strikes, and he calls and asks for help. Sometimes there is no record of any prior connection at all. We do everything we possibly can. We scramble in order to build those relationships, right there in the moment, that day. But I always wish that those relationships and connections had been put firmly in place long before the grief-stricken call. As Christians, we need never grieve alone. We have brothers and sisters in Christ who are part of the family of God. We will grieve together.

In the storm of grief

So what are we going to do? We're Christians, and we want to act like Christians not only in the best of times but also when times are dark.

Grieve your loss. Jesus did. Read John 11. When one of his best friends, Lazarus, died, Jesus went to his tomb, tears flowing. So great was his grief that bystanders stopped their own crying, overwhelmed by his tears. We need not stifle or hide our weeping. Don't get the idea that Christians need to suppress grief in order to make a good impression. Sometimes, by pushing grief underground, we establish a toxic waste dump that is going to bubble up at some future date. It is far better to deal with it upfront.

Accept help. God channels grace to us through others. You may be inclined to go it alone. I'm one of those people, too. I think, "I have enough trouble managing my own emotions without having to deal with the emotions of other people. I'll just go off by myself and tough it out." However, prolonged isolation is seldom good. We need counsel and encouragement. We need the experience, wisdom, touch, and love of other Christians. So let them help. Accept their calls. Let them stop over. When they want to listen, talk. Pour it out. Let it flow. Do what you need to do to accept the help of others. Let them be God's blessing to you and God's agents in the midst of your grief.

Serve others. Psychologists tell us that when we are in the deepest pit of difficulty, one way to crawl out of that pit is to serve others. But long before modern psychology and counseling books were written, we have the words of 2 Corinthians 1:3-4. *"Praise be to the God and Father of our Lord Jesus Christ, the Father of compassion and the God of all comfort, who comforts us in all our troubles, so that we can comfort those in any trouble with the comfort we ourselves have received from God."* God gives comfort, blessing, and grace to us both directly and through others. We can let it flow through us and out. Even when we are grieving, we can bless and benefit others who are in the midst of difficulty.

Grieve with hope. Most of all, we act like Christians by holding onto our hope. Act out your Christian faith by affirming that hope, even in midst of grief, declaring that you believe in God. Actually tell God that. Trust Jesus for eternal life, and trust him to get you through whatever you are now going through. That can be difficult to do in the middle of grief. But it is a very good time to renew your love and loyalty to Jesus Christ. It is absolutely the wrong time to distance yourself from God. In grief we want to be as close to God as possible.

Hope is the expectation of a better tomorrow. It is trusting God. It is saying that if God can forgive our sins and guarantee us heaven, God can get us through absolutely anything. As Christians, we can even look death in the eye and be assured of a resurrection and eternal life that has been promised by God. Through Jesus Christ, there is always a better future.

Hold on to God

When we are sinking so deeply into grief that hope is slipping through our fingertips, when hope is out of our grasp and we've given up on God and life itself, God does not give up on us. God is there for us, caring for us. God is present, even if we do not acknowledge God. God holds onto us until we can once again grasp the eternal hope that God offers.

Part Four:
Christian Character...
Growing in the
Hallmarks of Faith

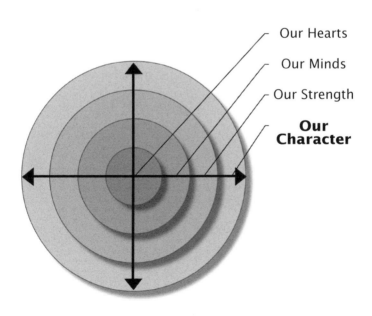

Our Hearts

Our Minds

Our Strength

**Our
Character**

Living with a Purpose in Life

Wouldn't it be great to know our purpose in life beyond even the tiniest, nagging doubt? Perhaps it would be best if we received a certificate at birth that stated exactly why we had been born and what we were supposed to do with our hours on earth. It would make life a lot clearer and more efficient. We'd know what schools to attend, what people to meet, what internships to pursue, and how to spend our time for maximum achievement.

I have heard people who had an admirable degree of clarity on the topic:

- "I was born to be a mother. My life is all about giving birth and raising children."

- "My purpose in life is to have a good time. 'Eat, drink, be happy, and die'—that's my motto."

- "The reason I'm on earth is to improve the world and leave it a better place than when I was born."

I once heard a man say that he knew in the first grade he would be a surgeon, marry a blue-eyed blonde, and have five children. Today he is a fifty-year-old surgeon married to a blue-eyed blonde (who was a student in that same first grade class), and the father of five children spaced exactly five years apart.

The search for purpose

But that kind of certainty is rare. The majority of people are more likely to say, "Life has turned out completely different than what I predicted or hoped for. I'm still searching for my purpose in life."

In pursuit of some clarity and peace in this area of life, people devour books and attend seminars. Yet most of these devout students *still* don't know their reason for being alive.

As Christians, knowing our purpose on earth seems particularly important. We have a desire and a drive to accomplish all that God has laid out for us. So why isn't it easy to find that purpose? In the Bible we see examples of people who were given their exact plan and purpose. Take a look at Matthew 1:18-21, for instance.

> *This is how the birth of Jesus the Messiah came about: His mother Mary was pledged to be married to Joseph, but before they came together, she was found to be pregnant through the Holy Spirit. Because Joseph her husband was a righteous man and did not want to expose her to public disgrace, he had in mind to divorce her quietly.*
>
> *But after he had considered this, an angel of the Lord appeared to him in a dream and said, "Joseph son of David, do not be afraid to take Mary home as your wife, because what is conceived in her is from the Holy Spirit. She will give birth to a son, and you are to give him the name Jesus, because he will save his people from their sins."*

The angel made it clear. Joseph's purpose was to marry Mary and be Jesus' father. Mary's purpose was to mother the Son of God. Jesus' purpose was to "save his people from their sins."

But when was the last time an angel appeared to you with a proclamation? We need to work with the information and help that we have.

Doing the research

God cares about you and wants you to know your purpose in life. God doesn't intend to leave you foundering, but deeper investigation may be in order. We'll take advantage of clues that lead to insight, starting with "four P's":

- Purpose—Why I am alive

- Preference—What I like

- Person—Who I am

- Plan—What I'm going to do

This list isn't definitive, but it serves as a kick-start to discovery.

Purpose: Why I am alive. "My purpose" is another way of saying "This is the reason I was born." It answers a basic human question and directs me in what I am to do with my limited time on earth.

When we become Christians, our purpose options dramatically change and enormously narrow. We become God-centered instead of self-centered.

This is totally counter-cultural. Listen for a moment to the less-than-subtle messages around us about what makes a person valuable in our society and what they are to pursue in order to be considered successful. We are bombarded with messages that say it's all about us and what we want: our happiness, our needs, and our fulfillment. The messages insinuate that if we choose anything else, we're less than successful. Self-help books are a multi-billion dollar industry. There's nothing wrong with improving our lives, but it's a sideline at best and a distraction at worst.

As Christians who have pledged love and loyalty to Jesus Christ, our purpose is not about us: our bodies, our looks, our wealth, our education, or our jobs. We live to please God. Sometimes that purpose runs contrary to the pursuit of self-improvement. It always runs contrary to self-absorption.

Preference: What I like. Preference is the way I would like my life to be, the dreams I want to come true. The list of preference possibilities is as diverse as the people who inhabit the earth. Some of the more usual choices include good health, a great job, wealth, marriage, children, and happiness. People may strive after a college education, a summer home in California, an expensive wardrobe, friends in high places, or opportunities to travel. Our preferences can be grandiose: a professional sports contract, a book deal, a hit album, an Academy Award, or a Nobel Prize. They can be basic: having the resources, funds, and health to live independently. They can be altruistic: finding a cure for cancer, serving in the Peace Corps, becoming a missionary, helping anyone in need who crosses our path. They can be dark: getting even with people who have hurt us, or using others to get what we want.

Dreams are our preferences imagined as if they were reality. It's wonderful to dream. Some preferences are reasonable and reachable. Others are totally farfetched and extremely unlikely to be fulfilled. In America and other wealthy Western countries, one of the most frequent misperceptions we have (and teach our children!) is that "you can do anything you want to do; you can be anything you want to be." The truth is that we cannot have everything we desire, no matter how privileged we are.

Person: Who I am. I have a fairly definite idea of who I am. I am a male who was born into a middle-class family with an immigrant mother and a father who was raised in working class poverty. I have three older brothers. My aptitude in music, sports, and foreign languages is minimal. I'm good at learning (if I work hard). I enjoy people, communication, and leadership.

Who are you? What are you good at? What are your strengths? Sometimes the person and preferences align, but for many of us there is a disconnect. Albert Einstein wanted to be a concert violinist but was better at physics and math. The apostle John wanted to be a politician seated at the right hand of the king, but he was better at writing five of the New Testament books. Esther wanted to retire into the safety and comfort of being queen, but she was really good at courageously saving the Hebrew people, her people, from genocide.

Plan: What I'm going to do. My plan is a list of specific actions to take so that I can take advantage of (or overcome) who I am, satisfy my preferences, and fulfill my purpose. These are the steps I'm going to take during my life. Having a plan means I'm actually doing something.

Living with a purpose—getting started

To begin living with (or figuring out how to live with) a purpose, try a few practical suggestions.

(1) Write a purpose statement. Corporations do it to keep them-selves focused—why not you?

Get started. Just finish this statement, "The purpose of my life is to...." Keep it short, simple, and personal. Most impor-tant of all, keep it God-centered. At the heart of your state-ment is the recognition your life as a Christian is all about God and not all about you.

Write a statement that fits you now but will still fit next year and the next and on and on into the final year of your life. Start today. Revise tomorrow. Reword next week. Pray for God's help. Getting a purpose statement into words can be fun, but it can also be very hard work. Understand that if you do a good job of this, your purpose statement will shape and direct the rest of your life.

Here are a few examples:

- The purpose of my life is to glorify God and enjoy God forever.
- The purpose of my life is to make God look good.

- The purpose of my life is to please Jesus Christ every day.

- The purpose of my life is to point people to God.

- The purpose of my life is to bless others in Jesus' name.

- The purpose of my life is to be a consistently godly person.

Think about the power of making a statement like that and putting it in writing. Hang it on the mirror. Have it framed. Memorize it. Think through the actions of your life in terms of your statement. It may change everything!

(2) Dream your preferences. If you could have whatever you want, what would that be? Fame? Fortune? Life on a farm? Marriage? A career as an astronaut? Dreaming is an important part of the purpose process. Sort through those items and consider how they fit with your purpose statement. Are there preferences that will interfere with the achievement of your purpose? How can your preferences contribute to the fulfillment of that purpose?

(3) Describe yourself. On paper or in your head, make a list of who you are and what you've got to work with. Include the best and the worst. Include gender, age, education, strengths, weaknesses, abilities, disabilities, family, friends, education, assets, liabilities, and whatever else describes you. The list doesn't have to be long, but it should be honest. If you are eight years old, you probably have a lot of future possibilities to consider; if you are eighty, you have plenty of rich history from which to draw plus some time limitations.

Consider who you are as a gift from God. You are uniquely you, and God wants you to live *your* life, not someone else's. It's a sad thing to say, "I wish I were somebody else," because we can't be anybody but who we are. Of course we can overcome obstacles and strive to be our best. But God has made you to be you and not another person. At the end of your life, God won't ask you why you weren't

Moses, David, Esther, Mel Gibson, Wayne Gretsky, Sandra Day O'Connor, or Bono. God will ask you only about you.

(4) Pray about it. Look at Psalm 37:4-7 as a basis for a prayer about living with purpose:

> *Take delight in the LORD*
> *and he will give you the desires of your heart.*

Put God first, no matter what. Whatever God wants should be our choice, too, even when that choice means our preferences aren't met. We aren't guaranteed the items on our preferences list, but God can change those desires and help us to prefer what is best.

> *Commit your way to the LORD;*
> *trust in him and he will do this:*

We can have absolute confidence that God will accomplish God's purposes in our lives if we remain committed to the Lord.

> *He will make your righteous reward shine like the dawn,*
> *your vindication like the noonday sun.*
> *Be still before the LORD*
> *and wait patiently for him;*
> *do not fret when people succeed in their ways,*
> *when they carry out their wicked schemes.*

Trust in God's schedule. Don't worry if the people around you appear to be achieving more and receiving all the accolades. We don't need to compare. We only need to trust God.

What would our prayer sound like? Perhaps something like this: *"God, the purpose of my life is to please you. I commit to making you number one in my life. You made me and know me. I trust you to fulfill your purposes in me even*

if that means giving up my preferences. I'll leave the tim-
ing to you. I may die without knowing all that you have
planned or will accomplish, but I give my life to you. In
Jesus' name. Amen."

(5) *Choose a plan.* Go ahead and make a plan for your life. Consider school, career, money, and family. Make certain everything you choose helps you fulfill your purpose. If the purpose of your life is to please and honor God, how will you uniquely do this in the way you choose your job, spouse, education, budget, car, friends, parties, clothes, and employment? How will your purpose affect how you deal with business acquaintances, the treatment of poor people whom you encounter, the Internet, your expense account, politics, reading material, sports, and children? How will your purpose affect things that surface unexpect-edly during your lifetime—things you would never choose; things you don't want to think about even now; things like cancer, divorce, bankruptcy, violence, and natural disas-ters?

(6) *Check your progress.* Make check-ups part of your routine. Ask yourself frankly, "How am I doing in fulfilling my pur-pose?" Realize that you're not in this all alone. God is fulfill-ing a divine purpose in you, too.

There is an amazing and supernatural teaching in Romans 8:28-29: *"And we know that in all things God works for the good of those who love him, who have been called accord-ing to his purpose. For those God foreknew he also predes-tined to be conformed to the image of his Son..."*

In other words, we're not the only ones with a purpose and a plan. God established both for us before we were born. God is working to make everything come together for good, even our mistakes. God's plan is to make us like Jesus. Check in occasionally and realize all that God is doing.

(7) *Change the plan.* What if I decide to glorify God as a parent but never get married or have a child? It's time to rethink

the goal. How can I, instead, glorify God while being single and without children? If I plan to please God in my job but get laid off, the plan needs to change so I can dedicate myself to pleasing God as someone who is unemployed at the present time. If I plan to make God look good and suddenly find that I am restricted by unexpected sickness, how can I fulfill my purpose and make God look good even while I am ill?

Bethany Hamilton was ranked as the best amateur teen surfer in Hawaii. She was attacked by a tiger shark and lost her arm in October 2003. A fervent Christian, she had planned to fulfill her purpose through competitive surfing. She told her father that if having only one arm meant she'd never reach the top in competitive surfing, then she would look into playing soccer.[27]

Like Bethany, we may suddenly confront obstacles that change our worlds. Our plans may change but our purpose will remain steadfast.

What do we need to stay focused?

St. Paul showed us what it is like to live with the purpose always in mind. In Philippians 4:12-13 he writes, *"I know what it is to be in need, and I know what it is to have plenty. I have learned the secret of being content in any and every situation, whether well fed or hungry, whether living in plenty or in want. I can do everything through him who gives me strength."*

Paul said, *"I can do everything,"* but he didn't mean that he could buy a mansion in Rome when he was broke or that he could magically make sandwiches appear when he was hungry. Instead, he meant that he could change his plan and fulfill his purpose for God even when his circumstances changed. A few lines later he added, *"To our God and Father be glory for ever and ever. Amen"* (Philippians 4:20). That is exactly what it's all about.

Circumstances change. Bethany lost an arm. Paul went to prison. We get older. But God stays the same, and our purpose stays the same. We live to please and honor God no matter what our circumstances are, no matter how our preferences are dashed, no matter what.

Do it "on purpose"

When I was an eight-year-old third grader, I walked the one-mile distance from school to home each day for lunch. One afternoon I quickly ate my lunch and then headed out in the back yard to play with my dog. I took the dog's leash and started spinning it around as fast as I could make it go. This proved to be great entertainment. When it was time to walk back to school, my mother called out to me, and I stopped the leash. It snapped around, and the metal hook squarely hit and split my front top tooth. I intuitively caught the pieces and ran into the house. I was driven to the office of Dr. Stillwell, our family dentist. With tears running down my cheeks I told him, "I didn't do it on purpose."

That was my favorite excuse every time I did something stupid, but it was very true. To this day I'm still missing the back half of my front tooth, and I want you to know that I didn't do it on purpose.

The practical question for Christians isn't what we *don't* do on purpose. Instead, it is what we *will* do on purpose. Let us think through every day how we can purposefully, thoughtfully, intentionally, and deliberately live our lives to please and honor God—on purpose.

Chapter Eleven

Praying that Makes a Difference

I had forgotten about Hank, and that's not surprising because I never actually knew him. His mother, a woman in a church where I once was a member, is the memorable one. She had a habit of asking me to pray for her adult son, and not just once or twice. Repeatedly. Constantly. If I saw her coming, I knew that sooner or later she'd get around to asking me to pray for Hank.

She didn't just buttonhole me; she asked anyone she came into contact with, anyone who had ever shown the slightest inclination to pray about anything. We could count on her. At every small group gathering, every church prayer meeting, and in every social conversation, she requested prayer for her prodigal son. It became embarrassing and (we admitted silently to ourselves) annoying. Worst of all, her incessant requests and our constant prayer seemed to make no difference in Hank's life. He showed no spiritual inclinations and never came to church. Secretly, many people felt that praying for him was a waste of time. This man's mind was already made up. He was a lost cause.

But I remembered both Hank and his mother when I ran into this mother's former pastor. This pastor had met the woman forty years earlier. On their first meeting she had asked him to pray for her son, and the pastor had been asked time and again to pray for Hank in the years following. The story was the same: constant prayer, no results. After decades of service, the pastor retired and moved west. He searched for a church home in his new community. While visiting a new congregation, a stranger approached him and said, "Aren't you my mother's former pastor?" It was Hank. Not only was he attending church, but he was also deeply devoted to Jesus Christ and served as an elder of the church. The prodigal son had repented and come home to Jesus. His life had been transformed. His faith was alive and vibrant. It took longer than his mother's lifetime, but her persistent prayers were answered. The promise of James 5:16 proved true. *"The prayer of a righteous [Christian] is powerful and effective."*

How well do we pray?

Of course, prayer is not the exclusive domain of loving mothers. Prayer is part of many religions and at one time or another just about everyone in the world prays. One *Newsweek* article stated that 64 percent of Americans say they pray every day.[28]

But that statistic doesn't say much. Just about everyone eats, too, yet some people eat garbage and others gorge on gourmet cuisine. Some walk with stumbling steps while others run marathons. Some sing like opera stars, and other sound like dying elephants.

The same variation is found in prayer. Some people pray only when faced with calamity. Some robotically pray before each meal, without thinking much about what they're saying. As Christians, we want to pray well, to have our prayers mean something and make a difference.

A prayer primer

We can tap into a whole library of books written on the topic of prayer. There are so many books available, there is so much to learn about prayer, and there is so much to experience in practicing prayer that an individual searching for answers may feel more overwhelmed than instructed! Let's look at a few basics of prayer in order to improve our prayer lives.

Principle #1: Prayer is communing with God. Although even knowledgeable Christians often use the word *pray* as a synonym for *ask*, prayer is not mostly about asking. Nor is it mostly about talking. Prayer is connecting to God. An even better word than *connecting* is *communing.* There is powerful, personal communication that takes place between God and a Christian who prays.

Compare prayer to the communion that takes place between a parent and a child. Before birth a mother and child are physically connected. The baby hears and recognizes the parents' voices even before birth. After birth, there is a bonding that is physical, spiritual, and indescribable. Communication occurs through eye contact, body language, touch, and even through the parents' responsive meeting of the needs of their infant. Soon, words and then conversation is added to this mix. Around the age of two, a child's questions begin to flow. (Some parents might compare this development to the gushing of a fire hydrant!) By adolescence, there are piles of requests from "Is it okay to stay out late?" to "May I use the car?" Then as the relationship matures, there are fewer petitions and a deeper communication. It may even come to a point where the child parents and the parent is like a child—where a grown son holds a dying mom's hand in the hospice bedroom. All of this is a lifetime of relationship that goes far beyond communication and is better described as communion—the touching and intertwining of lives. Sometimes that communion speaks, but often it is silent.

So it is with prayer. We connect with God. Sometimes we ask questions, request directions, and even plead for help. But other times we say nothing; we sit in God's presence and listen, silently enjoying God's company. So prayer is an experience that is manifested in many different ways. The Bible describes these experiences and variations of prayer:

"Be still, and know that I am God" (Psalm 46:10).

*"Shout for joy to the L*ORD*"* (Psalm 100:1).

Jesus said, *"My sheep listen to my voice; I know them, and they follow me"* (John 10:27).

"If you believe, you will receive whatever you ask for in prayer" (Matthew 21:22).

Prayer is shouting, singing, and silence. Prayer is listening and asking. Prayer is communion with God. Christian prayer is not most about answers. It is most about God.

Principle #2: Prayer has a template. The template for Christian prayer is to address God the Father with the power of the Holy Spirit in the name of Jesus the Son. This is not a magic incantation, where the right formula guarantees the desired results, but it is the normative pattern for Christian prayers.

Check out the opening line in the Lord's Prayer (Matthew 6:9). Jesus calls on *"Our Father in heaven."* We can do the same.

Our prayers should also acknowledge the Spirit's power and presence. Romans 8:26-27 reminds us of the important role the Holy Spirit plays in prayer: *"The Spirit helps us in our weakness. We do not know what we ought to pray for, but the Spirit himself intercedes for us through wordless groans."*

And why end a prayer "in Jesus' name"? Again, there is nothing magical about this, but it is recognition that through Christ we have access to God the Father. Jesus provided a bridge to God by paying for our sins through death and resurrection. In John 16:23-24, Jesus talked about the future and told his followers, *"In that day you will no longer ask me anything. Very truly I tell you, my Father will give you whatever you ask in my name. Until now you have not asked for anything in my name. Ask and you will receive, and your joy will be complete."*

Principle #3: Prayer makes a difference. If we truly believe this, we'll never stop praying! Over and over again, the Bible offers evidence of the power of communing with God in prayer.

"If you believe, you will receive whatever you ask for in prayer" (Matthew 21:22).

"Do not be anxious about anything, but in everything, by prayer and petition, with thanksgiving, present your requests to God. And the peace of God, which transcends all understanding, will guard your hearts and your minds in Christ Jesus" (Philippians 4:6-7).

"And the prayer offered in faith will make them well; the Lord will raise them up. If they have sinned, they will be forgiven. Therefore confess your sins to each other and pray for each other so that you may be healed. The prayer of a righteous person is powerful and effective" (James 5:15-16).

"For the eyes of the Lord are on the righteous and his ears are attentive to their prayer" (1 Peter 3:12).

We sometimes struggle to accept God's promises about prayer as true. Yes, there are ample stories of the answers to prayer. We can read medical research about the connection between prayer and healing. We can see the results of secular polls that tell about peoples' answers to prayers. We can listen to anecdotes by the thousands and even the millions.

But we need to be cautious in our terminology, taking care that when we say, "Prayer works," "Prayer makes a difference," or, "It's an answer to prayer," we understand that it is *God* who makes a difference. Prayer is only the tool we use to connect us with the person and power of God. If I dial 911 and the paramedics rush to save my life, I don't give the credit to the telephone but to the paramedics. The phone is merely the instrument used to reach them.

Principle #4: Prayer takes discipline. Prayer doesn't just happen; at least it doesn't just happen well. If we want to pray like Christians, we need to remember that Jesus worked at prayer. He made prayer a priority, even walking away from crowds to keep his appointment with God. Jesus often prayed all night. Jesus took time to teach his disciples to pray. We can read in the Bible some of what Jesus prayed. It takes instruction and practice to learn how to pray well.

Lessons learned from Martin Luther

Martin Luther was the great sixteenth century German leader, reformer, theologian, writer, and founder of the Lutheran church. Read his biography, and you'll see that even by the type A business standards of twenty-first century corporate America, he dwarfed us with the schedule he kept and the work that he accomplished. Yet, even this extremely busy and effective leader spent as much as four hours in prayer every day, stating that he could never get all his work done if he prayed less! He was convinced that prayer was the bedrock for a productive life.

Even a very busy man needs to get his hair cut, and Martin Luther went to the same barber for over thirty-five years! His barber, Peter Beskendorf, knew that Martin Luther was a brilliant and godly person, so he once asked Martin Luther for a plan that would help an ordinary man to pray. Luther went home and wrote a thirty-four-page book dedicated to "a good friend, Peter, the master barber." The book was titled *A Simple Way to Pray,* and it is still available today. Martin Luther recommended that people have a set time to pray each day. He did it morning and night, saying, "It is a good thing to let prayer be the first business of the morning and the last at night."

The practice of prayer

Let's follow the recommendation of Martin Luther and consider practical actions we can take to improve our prayer lives.

(1) Set a time and place. Certainly we can and should pray any-time and anywhere, but it is also important to have a regular time and place. When is best for you? Are you one of those people who wakes up whistling? Prayer early in the morning before exercise, a shower, and breakfast may be ideal for you. Set the alarm half an hour earlier, and make a daily appointment with God at 5:30 or 6 AM. Are you a night person who enjoys the peace of a quiet, dark house or apartment? Perhaps your best time to meet God for prayer is just before bedtime. Shut off the TV, turn off the computer, and put down the book. Keep your scheduled meeting with God at night.

Now pick a place. For Jesus, it was usually on a mountain or in a garden. For me, it's a spare bedroom in our house. For you, it may be out in the garden, in the garage, or in your car. If possible, pick a place where you can be alone and where you have the freedom to pray out loud and in different positions (standing, sitting, kneeling, or even prone on the ground). Keep a Bible, pen, and notebook or journal in this special location. Most important, find a place where you can have a reasonable expectation of privacy.

(2) Listen to God. When you enter that place at your selected time, first listen to God. We are inclined to start speaking immediately in the first seconds of prayer, demanding the presence and the ear of God before we are willing to listen. So start with silence, and don't drive the agenda.

(3) Have a plan. Undisciplined praying quickly becomes repetitious, boring, and even meaningless. Adopt a simple plan and stick to it until you sense that the time has come to develop a different one. Perhaps we should look to Luther's plan. He suggested four parts to prayer: instruction, thanksgiving, confession, and petition.

- *Instruction*: Luther read and prayed the psalms. Then he prayed through The Lord's Prayer, the Ten Commandments, and the Apostles' Creed. It wasn't that he memorized and recited these words as some sort of chant, but he used them as a basis for his own prayers. For example, when he prayed, "Give us our daily bread," he would pray specifically for the baker in his village and the politicians in the area (who guarded the peace so the baker could bake the bread!). When he prayed, "Forgive our sins," he would confess his own sins, specifically naming them one by one. And when he prayed for forgiveness for "those who have sinned against us," he prayed for each one of his enemies by name.[29] Luther had a plan that was rooted in the Bible, the prayers of Jesus, and the doctrines of the church. His prayers were not random. They were disciplined.

You can try any or all of Luther's instruction ideas, or use a devotional book or a book of prayers. Starting out in this reverent and quiet way helps to focus your prayer on God and learn from him.

- *Thanksgiving*: Thank God for his blessings.

- *Confession*: Admit sins, and ask for forgiveness.

- *Petition*: Ask God for what you want.

After years of praying, I have my own system. I suppose you could call it the Leith Plan, and it works for me. I first worship God, and tell him I love him. Every day I commit myself to God again. I confess my sin. I offer my thanks for all of his blessings, stating them by name. I pray that God, by his Spirit, will help me to honor him that day. Almost every day I pray, *"May these words of my mouth and this meditation of my heart be pleasing in your sight, LORD, my Rock and my Redeemer"* (Psalm 19:14).

I have petitions. Every month I write a new prayer list in a journal. At the top of the page I write the month, and across the page I write the days of the month. After praying, I check off the days. My list varies but usually includes:

- *Family*: I pray for the people in my immediate family (their health, requests, needs and upcoming events).

- *Church*: I seek God's blessings on the church that I pastor.

- *Myself*: I request wisdom, godliness, and the help of the Holy Spirit.

- *People*: I pray for different people each day of the week. This seven-day cycle includes neighbors, co-workers, church leaders, and extended family. I also have a short list of people for whom I pray every day.

- *World*: I pray for my country and government leaders. I also pray for different missionaries each day. That gives me the opportunity to get specific about the particular challenges that individuals face as well as the goals and needs that they can address with God's help.

I keep a journal and note all answers to prayers in red ink along with the date. I love to page back through months and years and see the red notations. Do you keep a record of God's answers to your prayers? Try it, and you'll see God's consistent involvement in your life through years and decades.

My plan works for me, and you'll discover one that works for you, too. If after a period of time (it could be months, it could be years), your prayer life has become stale, then it's time for a new plan. Do your research, think creatively, incorporate music, ask others what helps them—do whatever it takes to keep the experience fresh. This is a daily opportunity to experience the supernatural.

(4) *Include others.* Private prayer is the cornerstone of our personal relationship with God, but we should expand our practice of prayer beyond the private realm to include others. Jesus prayed with his disciples. The early Christians held regular group prayer meetings. The New Testament is densely packed with requests for the prayers of fellow believers and instructions to pray for one another. How can you go beyond individual prayer to share prayer with other Christians?

- *Recruit others to pray.* Like Hank's mother, share your prayer concerns. Don't try to tough it out alone. One of the privileges Christians have is the power and comfort of others' prayers. If you have a prodigal son or daughter, ask other parents to pray for your child. If you have chronic pain, recruit one, two, or more godly people who will pray every day for the next thirty days that God will relieve your chronic pain. Do the same if you're facing a frightening diagnosis, and ask people to pray that God will give a favorable outcome to the prognosis that seems so bleak. If you need a job, recruit six people to pray every day for you to find work. If you are struggling with an addiction, find a prayer partner who will pray with and for you.

- *Reciprocate.* Offer to pray for others. Don't just say you'll do it. Do it! Make a commitment to daily prayer for your friend, co-worker or fellow sufferer. Write their names and needs on your list. As Christians, we care for one another, and we pray for one another.

- *Pray with others.* If you have not learned to pray out loud with other Christians, make it a goal to learn. For some people, praying in groups comes easily. For others, it is frightening to the point of paralysis. According to a *Newsweek* magazine poll, Americans feel closest to God when praying alone, and only 6 percent feel the strongest connection to God when praying with others.[30] My guess is that the number is low because too few try.

If you want to learn to pray with others, start by praying out loud by yourself. Connect with a veteran Christian who will teach you to pray out loud, or find another novice and practice. Join a prayer group. It's okay to listen for a while! When you're ready to try, don't feel that you need to impress anyone; just speak from your heart. Good news: you may find that the more time you spend in private prayer, the more at ease you will be with corporate (or group) prayer. You'll be communing rather than worrying about "performing" for others.

I can promise that you'll be blessed by the time you spend praying with others. You will discover a power and presence of God that is amazing. Jesus said, *"For where two or three come together in my name, there am I with them"* (Matthew 18:20). Jesus is there, listening, when we pray alone, but he adds an extra punch when we pray with one another.

(5) Grow in prayer. As we mature in our Christian faith and life, we should get better at prayer. Zealously oppose getting stuck (it is easy to do!) or making excuses. We need to take inventory by asking ourselves, "Am I getting better at praying?" Compare your experience now to a month ago, a year ago, or a decade ago. Is the discipline stronger? Is the intimacy with God better? Is faith larger?

Making a change

I conclude with a confession. I am not satisfied with my prayer life. Are you? I want closer communion with God. I want to pray more. I want to pray better. I want prayer to be a greater priority in my schedule. I want to be a Christian of prayer. With a combination of fear and excitement, I resolve to grow in my prayer life. I invite you to grow with me.

Chapter Twelve

Holding on to Hope

Besides the physical needs for food, air, water, and shelter, there's one thing that humans require in order to survive and thrive in life. Some people say that it's health, and others claim that it's happiness. But one thing beats them both: hope. No one can make it through life without suffering illness, and it would be impossible to be constantly happy. But, as Christians, we can hold onto hope. Always.

The Bible tells the stories of people of faith who did just that, throughout long lives and difficult times.

Simeon and Anna, symbols of hope

Simeon was a righteous and devout man who lived by faith, something that could not always have been easy to do, considering his circumstances. A cruel Roman army occupied his country. He had waited patiently all of his life for the Messiah who had been promised to the Jewish people, but he was an old man and had not yet seen the fulfillment of his dream. It had been many, many years since the promise of a Messiah had been made. There was controversy even among the religious leaders about the whole issue. Simeon continued to hold onto hope, believing with all of his heart that the Messiah would come.

Anna was either old or very, very old.[31] Her husband had died, and she had spent her life mostly alone. It is never easy to be elderly or lonely, but it was particularly difficult in a poor and primitive place like first century Israel. In that era, widows were the most vulnerable of women. They had little income, few rights and diminished respect. But Anna had the hope of a Messiah. She was waiting for the fulfillment of the prophecy, and throughout her life she held onto hope.

Although we don't always associate them with the nativity or the celebration of Christmas, Simeon and Anna are a part of the Christmas story. You can read about them in Luke 2:25-38:

Now there was a man in Jerusalem called Simeon, who was righteous and devout. He was waiting for the consolation of Israel, and the Holy Spirit was upon him. It had been revealed to him by the Holy Spirit that he would not die before he had seen the Lord's Messiah. Moved by the Spirit, he went into the temple courts. When the parents brought in the child Jesus to do for him what the custom of the Law required, Simeon took him in his arms and praised God, saying:

"Sovereign Lord, as you have promised,
    you may now dismiss your servant in peace.
For my eyes have seen your salvation,
    which you have prepared in the sight of all nations,
a light for revelation to the Gentiles
    and the glory of your people Israel."

The child's father and mother marveled at what was said about him. Then Simeon blessed them and said to Mary, his mother: "This child is destined to cause the falling and rising of many in Israel, and to be a sign that will be spoken against, so that the thoughts of many hearts will be revealed. And a sword will pierce your own soul too."

There was also a prophet, Anna, the daughter of Phanuel, of the tribe of Asher. She was very old; she had lived with her husband seven years after her marriage, and then had been a widow for eighty-four years. She never left the temple but worshiped night and day, fasting and praying. Coming up to them at that very moment, she gave thanks to God and spoke about the child to all who were looking forward to the redemption of Jerusalem.

Through good and bad times, through long years of waiting, Simeon and Anna clung to hope. What kept them going? Wishful thinking? Positive thoughts? The Bible tells us that it was something more.

Hope anticipates future good

Jerome Groopman, MD, a Harvard Medical School professor and the author of the book, *The Anatomy of Hope,* defines hope as "the ability to see a path to the future."[32] Even when caught up in the difficulties of life, people with hope can see a way out of the difficulties. Hope is all about tomorrow.

Simeon saw the pain in his nation. He grieved over the afflictions of his people. He yearned for consolation. There was no apparent way to escape the oppressive Roman rule. Many had tried. There had been isolated and organized insurrections, but the Romans had cruelly crushed them all. To most people, that political situation would have seemed like an endless trap, but Simeon saw a pathway to tomorrow through a Messiah sent by God. His dream was to live long enough to see this king come to Israel. Hope was Simeon's key to survival during brutal times.

Anna was older. She had been a widow more than ten times longer than she had been a wife. She had no prospects of future success. Her fate was set. If anyone had a reason to feel hopeless, it was this woman. But she was full of hope, and not just static hope but hope that showed itself in action. The Bible account of her life says that she worshiped every day and practiced the disciplines of prayer and fasting. She was convinced that God would send a savior, the child she envisioned as certain hope for the future.

Hope when we need it most

Today, we still need hope. Of course when life is easy and all of our dreams are coming true, we don't rely on hope. But, eventually, most of us struggle with pain, problems, and uncertainty. We wonder how we'll survive today, and we dream of thriving tomorrow. We need a path out of the mess we are in, a way beyond hopelessness. We need hope that helps us anticipate the good yet to come. The trouble comes when we don't know where to find it or what it really is. Hope is the cornerstone of the Christian faith and a wonderful gift to every believer who will accept it. What do we really know about real, deep-down, unshakable Christian hope?

Hope comes from God. Hope without God is merely wishful thinking. Dreaming up fantasies of a happy future is not Christian hope. Such illusions are little more than self-delusion. Just because we "Think Snow" or "Envision Peace" or "Want Money" doesn't mean that any of it will come our way.

Christian hope is different because it comes from God, not from our imaginations. Simeon's hope came from the Holy Spirit. Anna's hope sprang from the prophecies of the Bible. True hope isn't our imaginary yellow-brick-road; it is based on the person, power, and promises of God.

Hope surprises. Hope often comes as a surprise. Although they had some idea of the significance of their baby, Joseph and Mary were surprised. After a virgin birth, angel appearances, and the fervent worship of shepherds, you might expect that Joseph and Mary would be surprise-proof. But they were amazed at the words of Simeon and the predictions of what was to come: *"The child's father and mother marveled at what was said about him"* (Luke 2:33). That's the way hope in God and life with God works. God puts us on a path to tomorrow but surprises us with twists and turns that we would never expect.

The spiritual autobiography of C.S. Lewis, *Surprised by Joy,* reminds us that just when we think all is lost, God sneaks up with victory. Just when we think we have it all figured out, God takes us in exciting and unexpected new directions. Hope is, to put it succinctly, surprises from God.

Hope takes time. Hope is seldom quick. Simeon and Anna waited all of their lives to see their hopes come true. Sometimes the fulfillment of hope takes *more* than a lifetime. Simeon and Anna did not live long enough to see the baby Jesus grow to adulthood. They did not witness his supernatural miracles or hear his divine revelations. They weren't around for his crucifixion or resurrection. They waited in hope and lived long enough to experience the beginning of God's fulfillment of the prophecies. With God, there is always more for which to hope in the future.

Often the fulfillment of our hopes moves slower than we would choose. It most often comes in incremental bits and pieces, not all at once. But as Christians our hope is not in the calendar or the clock. Our hope is in the Christ. We're like Anna and Simeon, anticipating the future as a path that leads away from the difficulties of today and into the delights of tomorrow. We are convinced that God will come through no matter how long it takes.

How to hope like a Christian

It is a lie of Satan that everything in our lives is out of control and there is no way out. God gives hope to Christians. We can take steps to behave like Christians in the arena of hope.

Guard hope. Hope is a precious commodity that needs to be carefully guarded.

Colossians 1:23 warns us to *"Continue in your faith, established and firm, and do not move from the hope held out in the gospel."* There is an always-present danger that we will be nudged away from or knocked out of hope. Many things can steal hope from our lives: disappointment, disease, poverty, death, and divorce are a few. You can probably add more to this list. These are the situations in life that leave us feeling powerless and hopeless. What's been stealing your hope lately?

We may be our own greatest thieves of hope. Although we don't choose to feel hopeless, we can easily and thoughtlessly put our hope in the wrong person, possession, or circumstance. Money is a powerful temptation, often mentioned in the Bible. 1 Timothy 6:17 offers a warning: *"Command those who are rich in this present world not to be arrogant nor to put their hope in wealth, which is so uncertain, but to put their hope in God, who richly provides us with everything for our enjoyment."*

The Bible has much more to say about pinning our hopes on financial security. When we are rich, and by world standards many of us are, we are prone to assume that money is our protection and the path out of every problem. In reality, money can be fleeting, easily lost to unexpected life circumstances or decisions.

Money isn't the only trap. When we are in love, we trust that person to always be there to provide the happiness and hopeful future that we dream of. When we are in positions of power, we are likely to put our confidence in our abilities, influence, and connections. When we're healthy and strong, we somehow believe that we will never be seriously ill or hurt. But as Christians, we know that these blessings carry no guarantees for the future. We can lose our love, fall from power, or become disabled by disease or accident. Our hope must be in God. Money, people, power, and good health are not dependable, but God is. Hold onto Christian hope. Stand guard against the robbers of hope and the substitutes for hope in God.

Claim the promises of God. We can become proactive about hope and claim the promises of God. I found that the word *hope* appears one hundred and sixty-one times in our English Bible. I read each reference, delighting to discover all that the Bible says about hope. Reading these verses was a huge hope-builder all by itself.

Here's my recommendation: look at the index in the back of your Bible, buy a concordance, purchase a Bible software program, or find an online concordance, and read every promise from God about hope. It will encourage you and plant a small seed of hope in your soul that will grow.

Out of the many references, choose one or two of your favorites, and write them down. Post them on your refrigerator or in your car, or use them as your computer screensaver. Memorize them and recite them regularly. To jumpstart your effort, I'll give you a few possibilities (for more, refer to the Index of Hope on pps. 147–151 of this book):

Those who hope in the LORD will renew their strength. They will soar on wings like eagles; they will run and not grow weary, they will walk and not be faint.
(Isaiah 40:31)

"For I know the plans I have for you," declares the LORD, "plans to prosper you and not to harm you, plans to give you hope and a future. Then you will call on me and come and pray to me, and I will listen to you. You will seek me and find me when you seek me with all your heart."
(Jeremiah 29:11-13)

May the God of hope fill you with all joy and peace as you trust in him, so that you may overflow with hope by the power of the Holy Spirit. (Romans 15:13)

Through [Jesus] you believe in God, who raised him from the dead and glorified him, and so your faith and hope are in God. (1 Peter 1:21)

The early Christians were under constant assault and were often in grave danger of torture and death, yet they left behind evidence that they retained hope. You can see that evidence for yourself by visiting the catacombs beneath the ancient city of Rome. In the first half of the second century, Christians buried their dead underground in long tunnels. Picture tombs cut in rows in the walls, stacked one upon another. These catacombs go on for miles. When burying their dead, the Christians wrote words and symbols on the walls of the caves. The most common symbols were the cross, the fish, and the anchor. Despite hardship, they clung to their faith and expressed it through these simple markings.[33]

We have this hope as an anchor for the soul, firm and secure. (Hebrews 6:19)

In the midst of poverty, persecution, and death, they held onto their Christian hope in God's grace. Hope was and is the anchor of our faith. Nothing extinguished the hope of those early Christians. Nothing need extinguish ours.

Be patient. Simeon and Anna waited for a lifetime before seeing their hopes come true. Remember that hope is always about the future, about what we have not yet experienced, and about what God will do in his time. Don't give up easily. Don't surrender too soon. Don't think that God has forgotten. Hold onto hope with the conviction that God will do good no matter how long it takes. Romans 8:25 reminds us: *"If we hope for what we do not yet have, we wait for it patiently."*

Expect surprises. Expect surprises when God turns hope into reality. Remember that our hope is not in good outcomes, pleasant circumstances, or positive situations. Our hope is in God.

After several decades of life experience, I have learned that I would much rather trust God than myself. Some of my dreams were better left unfulfilled. Some of my prayers deserved a "No." God is infinitely better and wiser than I am, and I am learning to trust God's decisions. God is generous beyond my dreams, thoughts, or prayers.

Remember that hope is seeing a path to a better tomorrow. It's a way out of a lousy situation. With that definition in mind, read 1 Corinthians 10:13:

> *No temptation has overtaken you except what is common to all. And God is faithful; he will not let you be tempted beyond what you can bear. But when you are tempted, he will also provide a way out so that you can endure it.*

God promises to give us all the strength we need through whatever situation we face, always providing a path to a better tomorrow. Yes, we may be totally surprised by the path God asks us to walk. But when we know and trust God, we want to follow God on that path, regardless of our surprise and our own plans.

Keeping the lights on

My father-in-law died at home in the house his parents built when he was twelve years old. They bought it through the Sears and Roebuck catalog, and the parts were delivered by train to Clifton, New Jersey.

At Christmastime in 1994, my wife Charleen's parents put up an artificial Christmas tree in the dining room of that house. Her father had already been diagnosed with terminal cancer, and we all knew that it was probably his last Christmas. He died at home in April 1995, in a hospital bed positioned within sight of that Christmas tree that was never taken down. In fact, the tree was left up with lights burning for the next six years.

The tree and its lights became for the whole family a symbol of hope for tomorrow rooted in the memories of yesterday. Through her years of grief, her own illness, and eventual death, Charleen's mother insisted that the tree stay put and the lights burn bright.

May the lights of hope keep burning for you. When illness strikes, when loved ones die, and when you feel swamped with discouragement, hold onto hope. Don't let anyone talk you into putting out the lights of hope. Keep your hope bright through faith in the God and Father of our Lord Jesus Christ.

Chapter Thirteen

Walking by Faith

My schedule is electronically entered in my personal digital assistant (PDA). It is the digital successor to the annual appointment books I used for many years. After making the switch, I learned to appreciate my PDA as an amazing tool. I can look up where I was on any day this year or last year and even multiple years before that. Not only is my past recorded, but also the future is reserved. My October 11 birthday is entered in perpetuity and is noted every year into the future. For example, October 11, 2031 will be on a Saturday. I may be long gone, but I still have that day set aside to celebrate.

I've discovered that my PDA has other benefits. Not only have I entered appointments far into the future, but I've also typed in names, addresses, telephone numbers, and driving directions to places I am scheduled to go. All I need to do is look up any future date and time, and I could tell you where I will be, whom I will be with, and what I will be doing.

All of this is comforting to me because I like to see where I'm going. I like clear and specific directions. I like predictability and certainty. I don't like surprises.

But life isn't like that. In one week there was both a birth and a death in our family that could not have been noted ahead of time in my PDA. I had a haircut scheduled for Tuesday, but because of the unexpected events in my life, I missed it and had to go on Friday instead.

Living by sight or by faith?

As Christians, we are faced with a choice: how are we going to live out our lives? The normal, natural, human way to live is by sight. The supernatural, Christian way to live is by faith. There's a significant difference between these two outlooks.

Life by sight involves looking at the facts and then deciding what to do based on what we see. We read books, absorb billboards, scan newspapers, and watch news shows. We check out what people are wearing and what people are doing, and then we decide how to live. Seems like a wise, healthy way to do things, doesn't it? Of course! What other way is there?

The alternate reality, living by faith, requires trusting our invisible God more than our human senses. There is nothing more Christian than living by faith. In fact, to live without faith means that we are not Christians. *"Without faith it is impossible to please God, because anyone who comes to him must believe that he exists and that he rewards those who earnestly seek him"* (Hebrews 11:6).

Living by faith is living by what we believe more than by what we see. Think about what a difference that makes! When we look at the events and activities in our world, we see cruelty, chaos, and uncertainty, but we believe that God is in control and is crafting everything for good. Living by faith means choosing attitudes and actions based on what we believe about God even when those beliefs do not seem consistent with what we experience in our lives.

One person's journey of faith

To see an example of someone living by faith, take a look at Abraham, whose story is told in Genesis 11–25. Abraham had a good life underway in his hometown of Ur, but God promised him a better life in an unnamed land far away. Abraham was seventy-six years old at the time—no spring chicken! He and his wife Sarah, who was well past childbearing years, had never been able to conceive a baby, a fact that deeply saddened them both. But God promised that they would have a child and many descendents. *"I will make you into a great nation, and I will bless you"* (Genesis 12:2).

What was Abraham's response to this outrageous, counter-intuitive offer? He packed up and left, as instructed by God. He went on an adventure God designed for him.

Years went by, and still Sarah was childless. God reiterated the promise. *"Look up at the heavens and count the stars—if indeed you can count them.... So shall your offspring be"* (Genesis 15:5).

Abraham's response? He believed.

Another decade passed. By then, Abraham was ninety-nine years old and his wife, Sarah, was ninety. They had been promised offspring by God, but by then the notion seemed farfetched, even impossible. Yet God kept his promise. In her old age, Sarah conceived a baby named Isaac. Abraham's walk of faith resulted in joy beyond his imagination. Hebrews 11:8-12 gives the synopsis of Abraham's journey through faith:

> *By faith Abraham, when called to go to a place he would later receive as his inheritance, obeyed and went, even though he did not know where he was going. By faith he made his home in the promised land like a stranger in a foreign country; he lived in tents, as did Isaac and Jacob, who were heirs with him of the same promise. For he was looking forward to the city with foundations, whose architect and builder is God.*

> *By faith Abraham, even though he was too old to have children—and Sarah herself was not able to conceive—was enabled to become a father because he considered him faithful who had made the promise. And so from this one man, and he as good as dead, came descendants as numerous as*

the stars in the sky and as countless as the sand on the seashore.

Abraham did not live by what he saw but by what God said.

Abraham's faith in today's world

What does this old story mean for us? Is there a core truth that has practical value for life in this century? It's unlikely that God will ask any of us to move from Ur to Jerusalem, have children in our nineties, or spawn descendents that outnumber the grains of sand on the seashore. But, like Abraham, we can live according to what we believe rather than what we see.

What we see	*What we believe*
Life is chaotic	Life is purposeful
Money makes people happy	Holiness makes people happy
Promiscuity is okay	Chastity is best
Sin rules the world	God rules the world
There's much to worry about	We need not worry; God is in control
Death is the end	Death means heaven

As humans, we depend on our senses. We depend on common sense. We depend on science, polls, and cold, hard facts. God doesn't ask us to abandon any of these things and put our brains on hold, but he does require that, as Christians, we rely more on our faith than on what is obvious to our human eyes.

Two kinds of faith

We need to distinguish between two sorts of faith that are represented in the Bible: *saving faith* and *living faith*.

Saving faith is the conviction that only God can save us from sin. Our sin has separated us from God because God is holy. We must get rid of our sin to spend eternity with God. Saving faith is founded on the belief that what happens in this life determines what happens to us in the next.

Most religions are in agreement on this point but, unlike Christianity, they teach that people must be good in order to get to God. If individuals can just be good enough—do enough good deeds, pray enough times and worship often enough—then they can accumulate enough points to outscore their sin points and win heaven as the prize. The Bible, however, clearly teaches that sinners can never score enough good points to get close to God. God does it all, everything, one hundred percent of the work. Only God is holy. Only God has the power.

That's where Jesus comes in. Sent by God, he lived a perfect life and died as a human sacrifice so our sins could be forgiven. Only through Jesus can we get to God. Saving faith is not primarily about believing facts but about trusting Jesus. We depend on him completely rather than our own efforts to take care of our sins and bring us into God's presence.

I imagine dying and being taken before God. God asks why he should accept me into heaven when I'm a sinner who deserves to die and be banished forever. "Jesus," I answer. "I'm completely counting on Jesus. I have good actions in my life, but they would never pay the price for the sins I have committed. Jesus," I repeat. "He's all I have to depend on. Without him, I'm an eternal goner. All I have is him." That's saving faith.

Living faith is the same kind of total confidence in Jesus for right now. It's totally trusting him for life and then making my decisions, basing every action on trust in Jesus. Proverbs 3:5 says, *"Trust in the Lord with all your heart and lean not on your own understanding."* I rely on his knowledge, wisdom, and power instead of my own insight.

Humans do this in other areas of life. Early in our marriage, Charleen and I went to a family practice physician in Colorado who took good care of us. We depended on him for every medical issue, whether for routine checkups in his office or for the delivery of our children in the hospital. When one of our children had to be rushed to the emergency room, the admitting nurse recognized us and called our family doctor at home. He came in and took care of our child.

One day our doctor told us he was leaving his practice to enter an anesthesiology residency at the University of Colorado Medical School. We were sorry to lose him, and I'm sure it was a leap of faith for him to leave his well-established office and appreciative patients. But he had great trust and respect for the chair of the anesthesiology department whom he thought of as one of the very best.

Then, in the midst of these well-laid plans, there came a surprise. His mentor decided to leave the University of Colorado in Denver and move to Montreal. That was tough on our physician, who had already given up so much, but he took his wife and children and moved from Colorado to Quebec. His commitment and trust were not so much in the residency program at the University as in his medical mentor.

That's what living by faith is all about for a Christian. Our commitment and trust is not primarily in any church or program; it is in Jesus. He is our Savior and Lord. We go where he goes. We make our decisions based on our faith in him.

Actions to live by

How can we actively live by faith? We take action!

But isn't any proposal of action contrary to Christian faith? No. The Bible tells us that faith and action are connected to each other. James 2:17 says, *"In the same way, faith by itself, if it is not accompanied by action, is dead."* We can't really talk about one without recognizing the other as integral. So take action to build your faith!

Remember what God has done. One of the very best ways to live by faith is to remember what God has done in the past. This is a recurring biblical theme. God told the Hebrew people to celebrate the Passover every year to remember how they had been saved from Egyptian slavery. Jesus instructed his followers to celebrate communion to remember how he sacrificed his body and blood on the cross to save us from sin. The better we remember what God has done in the past, the more we will trust God for the present and the future. The God of Abraham and Jesus is our God too!

Now gather memories of your own. Remember the time God saved you from a near-fatal car crash, gave you a job, brought you and your spouse together in marriage, provided money, lifted your depression, or healed your cancer. It is a valuable exercise to sit down and think about God's faithfulness. Make a list. Write in a journal. Post a note. Tell a friend. Remembering God's great deeds in the past helps us to entrust our lives to him today.

Consider the facts. This may sound like totally contradictory advice, but it is actually good to take a survey of your situation. Get a sense of what walking by sight includes. Ask yourself what the options are. Then ask yourself, "Given these circumstances, what would be a faithless way to live? What would be a faithful way to live?"

When I was a university senior, the head of my major department sat me down in his office one day to talk about my future. He told me that I was being inducted into a national honor society with a set of Greek letters and suggested that I follow a career in this field. When I told him that I was thinking about attending seminary, he made it clear that it would be a waste. I seriously considered what he had to say. Looking at my options helped me to decide what living by faith meant for me.

Believe God. Tell God you absolutely, completely, unreservedly trust him. Tell God that you believe he can do anything in your life. If God wants to cure cancer, God can cure cancer. If God chooses to give a baby to a couple in their nineties, God can make Sarah pregnant by Abraham. If God decides to fix the most shattered marriage imaginable, God can not only fix it but turn it into bliss. If God determines to do anything, God can do it—absolutely anything.

Tell God you know that he is good and right. Even if others refuse to believe in God, you believe. If some people criticize God as cruel, defend God as kind. If circumstances make God look bad, keep believing that God is good. If life turns bad, do not waver in your conviction that God's ultimate outcome is going to be good. Remember that living by faith presupposes faith and trust. Believe first, and then live out that faith by believing God.

Dream about what God might do. With your imagination rolling, just for fun, dream about what God might do. Hebrews 11:1 says that *"faith is being sure of what we hope for and certain of what we do not see."* So, start thinking and hoping for what God might do, and pray that God will direct your thoughts.

As long as your dreaming is God-focused, it can be an exercise of faith. Ephesians 3:20 pays honor to God *"who is able to do immeasurably more than all we ask or imagine, according to his power that is at work within us."* Truly believing changes how we think about possibilities. God can do anything.

Don't worry. Worry decreases as living by faith increases. That is not to say that we won't be concerned about our world, our families, our friends, and the details of our lives. But it is spiritually unhealthy when we obsess about our control over circumstances that should be entrusted to God. Philippians 4:6-7 commands us:

> Do not be anxious about anything, but in every situation, by prayer and petition, with thanksgiving, present your requests to God. And the peace of God, which transcends all understanding, will guard your hearts and your minds in Christ Jesus.

A very practical way to live by faith is to make a list of worries and entrust them to God. If you are a world-class worrier, you may need a notebook to write down all of your worries. Prioritize your top ten. Then pray and give them to God. Ask God how to live by faith rather than worrying. Give God some time to work this great miracle in your life, but expect God to take over your list.

Practice living by faith. Don't expect to zoom from low-level faith to Abrahamic faith all at once. Pick a few areas of life and get started on building up your faith. Start with something simple and grow upward. Where can we begin? With this short list of human concerns, play a bit of word association. Read the word, and listen for the Holy Spirit to provide a way that you can live by faith in that area of your life.

- Prayer
- Vacation
- Poverty
- Anger
- Missions
- Enemy
- Children
- Neighbors
- Car
- Money
- Health
- Church
- Sex
- Television
- Parents
- Job
- School
- Bible reading
- Politics
- Family
- Internet
- Discouragement
- Friends

Begin by living by faith in one, two, or three of these areas of life. You'll find that your expanding faith will grow to cover more and more areas of your life.

Just one person

We've seen how Abraham lived by faith, but you may think, "That was thousands of years ago. Abraham was a spiritual giant, a hero, and a paragon of faith. Real people can't live on the edge like that or trust like that." But people of faith are all around us, living and trusting God regardless of their circumstances.

I knew a man who grew up in a poor family near Philadelphia. His parents didn't even have grade-school educations. His father was a laborer in the shipyards who wasn't even sure of his age since his date of birth was never officially recorded.

This man had a serious speech impediment. He stammered so much that he dropped out of school when he was sixteen, without a high school diploma. Even without the diploma, he had received more education than anyone else in his family had.

One day he heard the gospel of Jesus Christ and believed. He accepted Jesus as his Savior and the Lord of his life. That day he began living by faith and stopped stammering.

He had numerous jobs, eventually settling on a career as bank teller. He married a young immigrant woman who gave birth to three children in five years. When their third son was born, she died in childbirth. He was twenty-seven years old. He had gone back to high school at the age of twenty-one and gotten a diploma, and now his goal was to get a college degree. He worked two jobs and carried twenty semester hours. He had a five-year-old, a four-year-old, and a newborn. Life was difficult but he lived each day by faith, believing that God was in control, despite his circumstances. I came to know him well and never heard him complain about the difficulties he experienced.

This man continued to live by faith as God led him on an amazing journey. It took him a long time, but he eventually earned a degree from a Lutheran college, went to seminary, studied at Princeton, became a pastor, served as president of a college, and touched the lives of thousands of people. Each of his grown sons eventually entered some type of Christian ministry—in overseas missions, higher education, or as pastors.

Looking at the circumstances of his life and the hardships he faced, it would be difficult to predict a positive outcome. In fact, seeing the facts would surely have made any observer certain that this was a young man headed for difficulty and disaster. But he lived a life of faith, based on *"what we do not see"* (Hebrews 11:1). It was a life of trust in God *"who is able to do immeasurably more than all we ask or imagine, according to his power that is at work within us"* (Ephesians 3:20).

That man was my father.

If we lived only by sight, we would not be Christians. By faith, we completely and unreservedly believe that God always does what is right for us. With the help of the Holy Spirit, we commit to live by faith, not by sight, through Jesus Christ our Lord.

Appendix

Index of Hope

Job 11:18 — *You will be secure, because there is **hope**; you will look about you and take your rest in safety.*

Job 13:15 — *Though he slay me, yet will I **hope** in him; I will surely defend my ways to his face.*

Psalm 9:18 — *But God will never forget the needy; the **hope** of the afflicted will never perish.*

Psalm 25:3 — *No one who **hope**s in you will ever be put to shame, but shame will come on those who are treacherous without cause.*

Psalm 25:5 — *Guide me in your truth and teach me, for you are God my Savior, and my **hope** is in you all day long.*

Psalm 33:18 — *But the eyes of the LORD are on those who fear him, on those whose **hope** is in his unfailing love,*

Psalm 33:20 — *We wait in **hope** for the LORD; he is our help and our shield.*

Psalm 42:5 — *Why, my soul, are you downcast? Why so disturbed within me? Put your **hope** in God, for I will yet praise him, my Savior and my God.*

Psalm 52:9 — *For what you have done I will always praise you in the presence of your faithful people. And I will **hope** in your name, for your name is good.*

Psalm 62:5 — *Yes, my soul, find rest in God; my **hope** comes from him.*

Psalm 65:5   *You answer us with awesome and righteous deeds, God our Savior, the **hope** of all the ends of the earth and of the farthest seas,*

Psalm 71:5   *For you have been my **hope**, Sovereign Lord, my confidence since my youth.*

Psalm 71:14   *As for me, I will always have **hope**; I will praise you more and more.*

Psalm 119:81   *My soul faints with longing for your salvation, but I have put my **hope** in your word.*

Psalm 130:5   *I wait for the Lord, my whole being waits, and in his word I put my **hope**.*

Psalm 130:7   *Israel, put your **hope** in the Lord, for with the Lord is unfailing love and with him is full redemption.*

Psalm 147:11   *The Lord delights in those who fear him, who put their **hope** in his unfailing love.*

Proverbs 23:18   *There is surely a future **hope** for you, and your **hope** will not be cut off.*

Isaiah 40:31   *But those who **hope** in the Lord will renew their strength. They will soar on wings like eagles; they will run and not grow weary, they will walk and not be faint.*

Jeremiah 14:22   *Do any of the worthless idols of the nations bring rain? Do the skies themselves send down showers? No, it is you, Lord our God. Therefore our **hope** is in you, for you are the one who does all this.*

Jeremiah 17:13   *Lord, you are the **hope** of Israel; all who forsake you will be put to shame. Those who turn away from you will be written in the dust because they have forsaken the Lord, the spring of living water.*

Jeremiah 29:11	"For I know the plans I have for you," declares the Lord, "plans to prosper you and not to harm you, plans to give you **hope** and a future."
Lamentations 3:25	The Lord is good to those whose **hope** is in him, to the one who seeks him.
Micah 7:7	But as for me, I watch in **hope** for the Lord, I wait for God my Savior; my God will hear me.
Romans 4:18	Against all **hope**, Abraham in **hope** believed and so became the father of many nations, just as it had been said to him, "So shall your offspring be."
Romans 5:2	And we boast in the **hope** of the glory of God.
Romans 5:5	And **hope** does not put us to shame, because God's love has been poured out into our hearts through the Holy Spirit, who has been given to us.
Romans 12:12	Be joyful in **hope**, patient in affliction, faithful in prayer.
Romans 15:4	For everything that was written in the past was written to teach us, so that through the endurance taught in the Scriptures and the encouragement they provide we might have **hope**.
Romans 15:13	May the God of **hope** fill you with all joy and peace as you trust in him, so that you may overflow with **hope** by the power of the Holy Spirit.
2 Corinthians 1:10	He has delivered us from such a deadly peril, and he will deliver us again. On him we have set our **hope** that he will continue to deliver us,

2 Corinthians 3:12	Therefore, since we have such a **hope**, we are very bold.
Galatians 5:5	But by faith we eagerly await through the Spirit the righteousness for which we **hope**.
Ephesians 1:18	I pray that the eyes of your heart may be enlightened in order that you may know the **hope** to which he has called you, the riches of his glorious inheritance in his people,
Ephesians 4:4	There is one body and one Spirit, just as you were called to one **hope** when you were called.
Colossians 1:23	Continue in your faith, established and firm, and do not move from the **hope** held out in the gospel.
Colossians 1:27	To them God has chosen to make known among the Gentiles the glorious riches of this mystery, which is Christ in you, the **hope** of glory.
1 Thessalonians 5:8	But since we belong to the day, let us be sober, putting on faith and love as a breastplate, and the **hope** of salvation as a helmet.
1 Timothy 4:10	That is why we labor and strive, because we have put our **hope** in the living God, who is the Savior of all people, and especially of those who believe.
Titus 2:13	We wait for the blessed **hope**—the appearing of the glory of our great God and Savior, Jesus Christ.
Hebrews 3:6	But Christ is faithful as the Son over God's house. And we are his house, if indeed

we hold firmly to our confidence and the **hope** *in which we glory.*

Hebrews 6:19   *We have this* **hope** *as an anchor for the soul, firm and secure.*

Hebrews 10:23   *Let us hold unswervingly to the* **hope** *we profess, for he who promised is faithful.*

Hebrews 11:1   *Now faith is being sure of what we* **hope** *for and certain of what we do not see.*

1 Peter 1:3   *Praise be to the God and Father of our Lord Jesus Christ! In his great mercy he has given us new birth into a living* **hope** *through the resurrection of Jesus Christ from the dead.*

1 Peter 1:21   *Through him you believe in God, who raised him from the dead and glorified him, and so your faith and* **hope** *are in God.*

Notes

1. In *1776* (New York: Simon & Schuster, 2005), David McCullough gives a compelling, nonfiction picture of the American Revolutionary War.

2. Jimmy Carter, *Sources of Strength: Meditations on Scripture for a Living Faith* (New York: Time Books, 1997), page xvii.

3. Mark Buchanan, *Your God is Too Safe* (Sisters, OR: Multnomah, 2001), p. 47.

4. Gordon Trowbridge, "Army Times," USA Today (November 22, 2004).

5. Focus on the Family, Citizen (July 2002), p. 12.

6. Marilyn Elias, "Psychologists now know what makes people happy," USA Today (December 9, 2002).

7. University of Michigan psychologist Christopher Peterson says that forgiving is the trait most strongly linked with happiness.

8. Jon Meacham, "From Jesus to Christ," Newsweek (3-28-05).

9. Tony Campolo, *Let Me Tell You a Story: Life Lessons From Unexpected Places and Unlikely People* (Nashville: W Publishing Group, 2000).

10. Ray Hoo, "Turn Your World Upside Down," Discipleship Journal (July/August 1982).

11. By permission of Rebecca Oehrig.

12. Jay Dennis and Jim Henry, *Dangerous Intersections: 11 Crucial Crossroads Facing the Church in America* (Nashville: Broadman & Holman, 2004).

13. "90 million adults talk about spiritual issues every day" *The Barna Group: The Barna Update* (6-9-03).

14. "Best Columns: The U.S.," *The Week* (8-12-05).

15. "Keep Sending Missionaries," *Baptist Press* (3-24-04).

16. Howard L. Dayton, Jr., *Leadership* (2:2).

17. It is challenging to translate money from one generation and culture to another, but there are some who may say that Jesus must have been using hyperbole—great exaggeration. Gold talents would have been worth many millions of dollars and would have exceeded the income and budget of many in the provinces of the Roman Empire.

18. Matthew 22:23-30 implies that the woman who died will be a woman in the resurrection in heaven. 1 Corinthians 15:49 indicates that Christians in heaven will have resurrection bodies similar to our original bodies on earth, just like Jesus whose gender apparently remains male.

19. Reuters (2-7-02).

20. For thorough information about the prevalence of pornography in our times, read "Internet Pornography Statistics" by Jerry Ropelato at www.internet-filter-review.toptenreviews. com/internet-pornography-statistics.html. There is also a "Christian statistics" component.

21. Rick Warren, *The Purpose Driven Life: What on Earth am I Here For?* (Grand Rapids: Zondervan, 2002).

22. *Our Daily Bread*, January 18, 2000.

23. Fred Smith, "The Care and Feeding of Critics," *Christianity-TodayLibrary.com*, 1997.

24. *Fresh Illustrations for Preaching and Teaching: From Leadership Journal,* edited by Edward K. Rowell, (Baker Pub. Group), 1997.

25. Jeffrey H. Boyd, "A Biblical Theology of Chronic Illness," *Trinity Journal* (24NS 2003), page 191.

26. *Ronald Reagan: An American Hero* (DK Publishing, 2001), pages 264-265.

27. Jill Lieber, "Teen Surfer Riding Wave of Amazing Grace," *USA TODAY* (March 19, 2004).

28. "Where we stand on faith," *Newsweek* (September 5, 2005), page 49.

29. Archie Parrish, *A Simple Way to Pray*, Fourth Edition (Marietta, GA: Serve International, Inc., 2005), 144 pages.

30. *Newsweek*/Beliefnet poll, *Princeton Survey Research Associates* (August 2-4, 2005). Survey results are available at www.beliefnet.com.

31. The Bible reports Anna's age in an ambiguous way. Depending on your reading of the Scriptures, she was either eighty-four years old or a widow for eighty-four years, which would mean that she was over one hundred years old by the time she saw the infant Jesus.

32. Rachel K. Sobel, "The Mysteries of Hope and Healing," *U.S. News and World Report* (January 26, 2004).

33. Stuart Briscoe, "Handling Your Insecurities," *Preaching Today*, Tape No. 119.